Is Your Fruit Sweet or Sour?

KAREN FINN

Precept
Publishing

Published by Precept Publishing, West Springfield, PA 16443
www.preceptpublishing.com

Cover and text design by Diane King, dkingdesigner.com

All Scripture is quoted from the Authorized King James Version.

Printed in the United States of America.

To my husband, Ted: I could not have done this without your support and encouragement! Thank you for your patience! I love you!

&

To my children: Ted, Brian, Dan, Katie and Kelly: Ditto!

Contents

INTRODUCTION

Have you ever bitten into a piece of fruit, expecting a sweet, satisfying savor, but discovered the portion you selected had a strong, bitter tang that surprised your taste buds? Yuck!

The fruit (or result) of our commitment to Christ can produce the same response. A Christian with a sweet testimony is pleasant to be around, while an individual with a sour spirit is one to avoid.

Is your conduct pleasing God? Maintaining an effective testimony as a teenager can be tricky *and* tiring! A wrong response, hypocrisy, peer pressure, selfishness…these are just some of the difficulties that will affect your spiritual walk. Perhaps it's time you re-evaluate what soft spots are setting in and damaging *your* fruit. Every now and then, your spiritual garden may need some pruning or watering. A fertile and healthy soul will require an attentive cultivator.

The themes that are covered in the first nine chapters are topics that will repeatedly taunt, tempt, or turn a Christian teen from fulfilling a life sold out to Jesus Christ. The last three chapters focus on results: the weeds have been pulled, yielding a lush and productive harvest.

Girls, you *can* have victory in those areas of weakness! Recognize your worth, realize your potential, and remain committed to honor God in all that you do.

> "That ye might walk worthy of the Lord unto all
> pleasing, being fruitful in every good work, and
> increasing in the knowledge of God." Colossians 1:10

NOTE TO READERS: All Scripture is quoted from the Authorized King James Version of the Bible. In instances where Bible references are given, the reader can utilize her preferred Bible translation for use and comparison. However, some questions or sections in the study may be difficult to complete, unless the reader is using a KJV Bible. In those cases, the answer key, available at: www.preceptpublishing.com, provides the desired response. Wherever possible, the author has defined an obsolete term for clarity and instruction.

What kind of fruit are you?

Before you begin the study, take a moment to complete the quiz. Circle which answer best fits the statement and seems to describe you best. Don't worry if some categories do not seem to "fit" your character! This quiz is meant to be fun, but may help to identify the soft spots in your life!

Category A. Total=_____

1. I won't admit when I have made a mistake or have been wrong about something.

5	4	3	2	1
always	usually	sometimes	rarely	never

2. I prefer to live by my own rules.

5	4	3	2	1
always	usually	sometimes	rarely	never

3. I don't like being told what to do.

5	4	3	2	1
always	usually	sometimes	rarely	never

4. I feel as though my parents don't know what they are talking about.

5	4	3	2	1
always	usually	sometimes	rarely	never

5. I hold my feelings in, whether they are good or bad.

5	4	3	2	1
always	usually	sometimes	rarely	never

Category B. Total=_____

1. I work hard for what I have, and I shouldn't have to share any of it.

5	4	3	2	1
always	usually	sometimes	rarely	never

2. I help out around the house (with chores) but only when asked.

5	4	3	2	1
always	usually	sometimes	rarely	never

3. I want to have what others have (cell phone, clothes, popularity, etc.).

5	4	3	2	1
always	usually	sometimes	rarely	never

4. When I am in a bad mood, others should sense it and leave me alone.

5	4	3	2	1
always	usually	sometimes	rarely	never

5. I don't like it when things don't go as planned.

5	4	3	2	1
always	usually	sometimes	rarely	never

Category C. Total=_____

1. I wish for things that I know I can't own or afford to buy.

5	4	3	2	1
always	usually	sometimes	rarely	never

2. My attitude is not one of gratitude.

5	4	3	2	1
always	usually	sometimes	rarely	never

3. I usually see the negative side of something before I see the positive side.

5	4	3	2	1
always	usually	sometimes	rarely	never

4. I long for how things "used to be" or imagine how they could be better.

5	4	3	2	1
always	usually	sometimes	rarely	never

5. I find it hard to trust God and believe that He is always in control.

5	4	3	2	1
always	usually	sometimes	rarely	never

Category D. Total=_____

1. I check with my friends first before I make a decision.

5	4	3	2	1
always	usually	sometimes	rarely	never

2. I want others to approve of me.

5	4	3	2	1
always	usually	sometimes	rarely	never

3. I am easily influenced by what others think or say.

5	4	3	2	1
always	usually	sometimes	rarely	never

4. I will do whatever it takes to be accepted.

5	4	3	2	1
always	usually	sometimes	rarely	never

5. I will give in to what others are doing, if it means avoiding a confrontation.

5	4	3	2	1
always	usually	sometimes	rarely	never

Category E. Total=_____

1. I like to have the last word in a disagreement.

5	4	3	2	1
always	usually	sometimes	rarely	never

2. I tend to hold a grudge against someone for much longer than I should.

5	4	3	2	1
always	usually	sometimes	rarely	never

3. I have a short fuse, when it comes to being patient.

5	4	3	2	1
always	usually	sometimes	rarely	never

4. I can go for a while without speaking to someone who has offended me.

5	4	3	2	1
always	usually	sometimes	rarely	never

5. I am easily upset when my expectations aren't met.

5	4	3	2	1
always	usually	sometimes	rarely	never

Category F. Total=_____

1. It's hard for me to keep a secret.

5	4	3	2	1
always	usually	sometimes	rarely	never

2. I share information with a friend and mask it as a "prayer request."

5	4	3	2	1
always	usually	sometimes	rarely	never

3. I speak out loud without thinking first.

5	4	3	2	1
always	usually	sometimes	rarely	never

4. I hurt others, not by what was said, but by the way it was said.

5	4	3	2	1
always	usually	sometimes	rarely	never

5. I will say something negative about myself in order to get a compliment.

5	4	3	2	1
always	usually	sometimes	rarely	never

Category G. Total=_____

1. I will compliment someone but not really mean it.

5	4	3	2	1
always	usually	sometimes	rarely	never

2. I point out someone else's faults but don't correct my own.

5	4	3	2	1
always	usually	sometimes	rarely	never

3. I want others to like me, so I will act like they do to accept me.

5	4	3	2	1
always	usually	sometimes	rarely	never

4. I will volunteer to do something, knowing it will make me "look good."

5	4	3	2	1
always	usually	sometimes	rarely	never

5. I act differently in private than what others see in public.

5	4	3	2	1
always	usually	sometimes	rarely	never

Category H. Total=_____

1. I don't see what the big deal is about being modest.

5	4	3	2	1
always	usually	sometimes	rarely	never

2. I don't like being held accountable for my actions.

5	4	3	2	1
always	usually	sometimes	rarely	never

3. It doesn't bother me when others use inappropriate language around me.

5	4	3	2	1
always	usually	sometimes	rarely	never

4. My texts, Facebook pictures and/or e-mails would not please the Lord.

5	4	3	2	1
always	usually	sometimes	rarely	never

5. I will use swear words or slang to impress someone.

5	4	3	2	1
always	usually	sometimes	rarely	never

Category I. Total=_____

1. I feel like I am missing out on a lot of fun when I have to follow the rules.

5	4	3	2	1
always	usually	sometimes	rarely	never

2. It's okay to tell a little white lie if I know that the truth will hurt.

5	4	3	2	1
always	usually	sometimes	rarely	never

3. My convictions for what I do or don't do are no one else's business.

5	4	3	2	1
always	usually	sometimes	rarely	never

4. I would rather not listen to someone else's opinion on an issue I am dealing with.

5	4	3	2	1
always	usually	sometimes	rarely	never

5. I would cover up for a friend who has done something wrong.

5	4	3	2	1
always	usually	sometimes	rarely	never

What kind of fruit are you? Scoring

Total your points for each category. Those with the highest amount of points could be the areas of concern that you may need to focus upon. Pay especially close attention to the chapter in this book that deals with the specific topic(s) of weakness and its weeds!

5–12 points: Good girl! Your testimony is quite balanced and trustworthy in this category. However, don't relax too much! Be on guard, knowing that "your adversary, the devil, as a roaring lion walketh about, seeking whom he may devour." (1 Peter 5:8)

13–19 points: Danger zone!! You probably hadn't realized how many dangerous influences and temptations were overtaking your attitudes and actions. Stay alert and proceed with caution.

20–25 points: You have seriously neglected to care for this area of your testimony. Pray for God's help and strength to address it and correct it . . . *immediately*! Ask for forgiveness and make a fresh commitment to the Lord!

DESCRIPTION OF EACH CATEGORY:

A. YOU ARE A COCONUT!

Your area of struggle concerns authority issues; the tough outer shell needs to go!

B. YOU ARE A WATERMELON!

Be alert to the selfishness you exhibit. It affects everyone and everything!

C. YOU ARE AN ONION!

Dry your tears! Discontentment wreaks havoc in your life, preventing abundant joy from flourishing!

D. YOU ARE A GRAPE!

Peer pressure dictates your habitat and habits, which usually rely on the "safety in numbers" philosophy!

E. YOU ARE A LEMON!

The way you respond shows a strong, sour side! Add sugar to make lemonade!

F. YOU ARE A PEACH!

The juicy drippings of a tongue misused are apparent in your testimony. Time to tame it.

G. YOU ARE A BEAN!

Your appearance is deceiving! Don't allow hypocrisy to be your trademark...work on being sincere.

H. YOU ARE AN APPLE!

Purity must reign throughout the very core of you! What sweet potential!

I. YOU ARE A CARROT!

Wrong influences are a blockade in your life. Work on clearing the path for true growth.

It's All About ME!

Selfishness

Agghhhhhh! I hate it when my sister wears something of mine without asking! Does she think I'm not going to find out!? She makes me so mad!! She is always ruining my things! I wish I didn't have to share my room with her!

Any teen girl who has a sibling—whether older or younger—recognizes this universal scene. The dispute may not be over clothing; perhaps it concerns toiletry items, jewelry, or personal space. But, does it really matter? Selfishness in any form can be a sin that snares us, making us stagnant in our walk with God. We succumb to its vise-like grip, never realizing the toll it will exact on those around us.

I discovered a good example for selfishness during a first-time gardening endeavor. I noticed that the watermelon was a *very* egocentric plant, crowding out the others with its curvy vine. The character flaw of selfishness develops in a similar way. Tendrils of self-absorption embrace our thoughts, guiding our actions and attitudes into their conceited grip. In a short time, priorities become shifted, and haughty excuses for our behavior begin to pile up.

John the Baptist declared in John 3:30: "He must increase but I must decrease." Under the ripe conditions (pun intended!), an inner desire to put Christ first will prevail over being in the spotlight. John was keenly aware of this principle and strived to point others to the coming Messiah and not to himself. We can all make a choice to follow his example!

Weed #1: Weed of Vanity

Characteristics: Portrays a prideful, prickly nature that persists and resists.

Caution! This wild plant has a tendency to grow out of control!

Cure? After pruning, immediately sprinkle seeds of humbleness in its place.

1. The concept of vanity is mentioned frequently throughout the Old and New Testaments. Look up these references to see what is being labeled as vain:

   ~ Jeremiah 4:14, 1 Corinthians 3:20 _____

   ~ Isaiah 36:5, Ephesians 5:6 _____

   ~ 2 Chronicles 13:7, Proverbs 12:11 _____

2. Keeping in mind that vanity is defined as **lack of real value, emptiness and/or worthless pleasure,** how can that lifestyle promote selfishness?

   _____

3. How does God handle the vanity that is in our lives? (Job 35:13)

   _____

4. What takes place in both 2 Kings 17:15 and Jeremiah 2:5?

   _____

   _____

   _____

~ The vanity in these verses can be equated with idolatry. When we act selfishly, what has become the object of our worship?

_____

5. List the sequence of behavior-related changes which occur in Romans 1:21–22 when the ungodly choose not to recognize or serve God:

~ a.) _____

~ b.) _____

~ c.) _____

~ What happens in verse 23? _____

_____

_____

6. In Matthew 20:28, what was Jesus' purpose for coming to earth?

_____

7. Read John 13:3–7 and 12–14. What action of servant-hood is illustrated here by Jesus?

_____

8. Paul instructs the members at the church of Philippi to look outward and be more concerned about others' needs than their own (Philippians 2:3–5). What will help us to develop that sort of outlook?

_____

9. When we take on the mind of Christ, His nature will be reflected in our lives. How is it possible for us to do this? (Refer to 1 John 2:6 and 1 Peter 2:21.)

    _____

    _____

10. Name as many qualities as you can that portray the mind of Christ.

    _____

    _____

    _____

    ~   Did you list vanity as one of these traits? _____

    ~   How many of these qualities describe you?

        _____

        _____

    ~   What areas do you need to work on, so that your (inner) mind and your (outer) conduct match up?

        _____

        _____

11. Continue reading Philippians 2:6–7. The expression "made himself of no reputation," in verse seven, refers to how Christ gave up His glory (as God the Spirit) when He took on the form of a man (God in the flesh). Christ literally abandoned self and exchanged it for human lowliness!

~ Interestingly, the Greek word for reputation in this context of Scripture, *keno*, means "to make empty." How does this differ from the emptiness of vanity?

_____

_____

_____

_____

_____

~ What form did Jesus "take on"? _____

~ Whose will does Jesus desire to follow in John 5:30?

_____

~ Can striving to have the mind of Christ also help us know God's Will for us?

_____

~ What attribute is certainly needed in order to accomplish this?

_____

THINK ABOUT IT:

I once heard a preacher say, "The quality of your life depends on the quality of your decisions." Which emptiness do you wish to choose: vanity or humility?

Weed #2: Weed of Rebellion

Characteristics: Mean-spirited and mighty; roots are tough and fibrous.

Caution! Can usually be found intertwined with weed of disobedience.

Cure? Incurable, difficult to prevent; erosion may occur under the right conditions.

Rebellion is an age-old rival. Ever since Lucifer's pride-centered fall from his exalted position, man's bent to choose self over God has been a recurrent theme. The progression goes something like this:

- God reveals Himself and His Law to man;

- Man initially obeys, but in due time, succumbs to his sin nature and rebels;

- God chastens (disciplines) and brings judgment;

- God forgives the repentant sinner(s) and graciously restores the relationship.

God's Word is abounding with individuals who opposed God's authority, *and* who sought to proceed regardless of the consequences. In this section, we will mainly focus on Saul's sin of rebellion, detailed in 1 Samuel 15:1–26. After reading the passage, answer the questions below:

1. What was Samuel's mission in verse one? _____

    _____

    ~   What is Samuel's *specific* instruction to Saul? _____

    _____

2. In verse three, Saul is told to attack Amalek. What details are given?

_____

_____

3. What does Saul do? (See verses 4–9.) _____

_____

_____

~ Was this 100% obedience? _____

4. What does Saul state in verse 13 that is a bold-faced lie?

_____

5. Saul continues to dig himself into a deeper hole! What excuse does he give for his rebellious response (verse 15)?

_____

How does he continue to justify this explanation (verses 20–21)?

_____

_____

6. Finish this quote from 1 Samuel 15:22: "Hath the Lord as great delight in burnt offerings and sacrifices as in obeying the voice of the Lord?

_____."
                                                    "

~ What does the Lord truly desire from us?

_____

~ Does this mean putting self or God first in our lives? _____

7. Saul admits his guilt in verse 24. What is his reason for disobeying God's command?

_____

_____

~ Do you think this is an acceptable explanation?

_____

~ Why or why not? _____

_____

_____

~ How was selfishness a motivating factor? _____

_____

_____

8. What happens to Saul's position as king in verse 26?

_____

_____

9. Why do the wicked not seek after God in Psalm 10:4?

_____

~   What view should we have instead (Psalm 119:97)?

_____

_____

10. We should seek to cultivate a thought life that puts God first. Read Joshua 1:7-8. How can the Bible's input and influence change our lives?

_____

_____

_____

_____

_____

11. God gave His people (us!) the Law to help them understand how to relate to their Creator and others, guidelines that are for our good and for His glory!

~   Write out the first commandment, found in Exodus 20:3.

_____

_____

~   How can submitting to this command keep you from displaying rebellion?

_____

_____

_____

Weed #3: Weed of Covetousness

Characteristics: A greedy, grasping creeping plant threatening to seduce or suffocate.

Caution! Too much watering can cause over-abundance of growth.

Cure? Thin gradually and carefully, fertilize with tenderness and compassion.

1. Covetousness is easy to diagnose, but not so simple to cure. That's because the problem begins as a deep-rooted issue. According to Mark 7:21, where does covetousness come from?

   _____

   ~ What other "issues" are mentioned that also come from the same place (verse 22)?

   _____

   _____

   _____

   ~ What will they eventually do (verse 23)? _____

   _____

2. Desiring worldly gain or things that belong to others is not only coveting, but a venue for selfishness, the essence of sin. Read James 1:14–15 and then answer these questions.

   ~ What does James say is responsible for this cause of temptation and enticement?

   _____

   ~ Who is in danger of being affected? _____

   ~ What happens once we give in? _____

~ How can we avoid this destructive outcome?

_____

_____

_____

3. The Greek words used for desire and lust, *epithumeo/epithumia*, can be interpreted as "to set the heart upon." They can also mean "to long for—especially for what is forbidden." In the following verses, identify what is sought after or desired, and tell whether it is something beneficial (good) or forbidden (bad).

~ Leviticus 19:31_____

~ 2 Chronicles 19:3_____

~ Job 31:35_____

~ Proverbs 17:11_____

~ Colossians 3:2_____

4. A covetous heart can mount into envy, discontent, and greed. As you complete the following chart, notice the object desired and what actions were undertaken to obtain it.

	Who is being covetous?	What are they coveting after?	Actions and/or Outcome:
1 Kings 21:1–4, 5–16			

	Who is being covetous?	What are they coveting after?	Actions and/or Outcome:
Esther 6:6–9, 10-12			
2 Samuel 11:2–4, 5-17			
Luke 16:14–15			

5. God realized the stronghold our desires can have upon us. What commandments are given in Deuteronomy 5:21 and Exodus 20:17?

_____

_____

6. Deuteronomy 27:9–10 shows that God has expectations for those that are "HIS", and that is to submit obediently to His commandments. On a scale of one (being most easy) to ten (being most difficult) how much of a struggle is it for you to obey the command to not covet?

_____

~ What area(s) of temptation and desire do you struggle with the most?

_____

~ What area(s) of temptation and desire do you struggle with the least?

_____

~ What solution for a covetous heart is given in Psalm 119:36?

_____

7. Inclining means "taking action"! And in this context, it suggests one who willfully yields or bends in the direction of. Who is there to guide us when we take action? (See Psalm 37:23 and Proverbs 16:9.)

_____

8. Following God's Law is symbolic of choosing the right path in life. What six things in 1 Timothy 6:11 does Paul instruct Timothy to follow after?

_____

~ Can these attributes be claimed by a selfish and covetous spirit?

_____

~ Which one of the traits listed is especially needful when it comes to obeying God's written Word?

_____

9. Identify the benefits of a heart which has sought after God and His Word.

~ 2 Chronicles 15:15 _____

~ Proverbs 28:5 _____

~ Jeremiah 29:13 _____

~ Amos 5:14 _____

10. It's okay to set your affection on something life-altering and permanent! Allow the psalmist's plea in Psalm 119:10 to guide your thoughts and actions. Write it out here.

_____

_____

_____

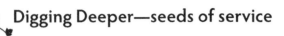

Digging Deeper—seeds of service

What do the three weeds of selfishness (vanity, rebellion and covetousness) have in common? They all lack the motivation to serve others! If we pour all of our energy into a self-centered agenda, it becomes impossible for us to make room for anything else! Nor do we care to.

Selfless and sincere hearts please a Holy God, and His pleasure should be the only recognition we should seek. He has provided us with the perfect instruction manual—the Word of God. When we heed its wisdom and its warnings, our character will become more like Christ's. Our lives won't be perfect, but they will have plenty of purpose!

Which path have you chosen to follow: the rugged road of arrogance and indulgence or the sturdy, distinctive trail of obedience and humility? Once we are on course, God will provide us with opportunities to minister and encourage, while repositioning our priorities. Let's abandon the world's ideology and acknowledge Jesus' words in John 12:26, "If any man serve me, let him follow me: and where I am, there shall also my servant be: if any man serve me, him will my Father honor."

Appearances are Deceiving

Hypocrisy

> Tall, blond, and beautiful Laura was a new co-worker of
> mine. She immediately attracted attention from all the
> guys in the office, and hardly spoke to the rest of us.
> My girlfriends and I assumed Laura was stuck on herself
> and talked about her behind her back.

Laura was not a snob, just a very shy person. I was offended by
Laura's lack of social skills, and thus, made unfair judgments about
her character. Laura never knew that I acted in such a backbiting
manner, because I put on a false face when around her, pretending to
be her friend. My misjudgment of Laura was not hypocrisy, but my
behavior toward her surely was!

I hope this kind of two-facedness doesn't exist in your friend-
ships. Appearances can be deceiving, meaning that what others see
may not always be the real deal! Are you pretending to be someone or something you're really not? When confronted, do you try to
conform and give the response expected? Have you considered your
motives and how they affect others? Eventually, this chameleon-like
tendency to please others will show its true colors.

The desire to be accepted by our peers will often influence our
actions and thoughts. We have to be careful that it doesn't become
the standard—or double standard—we live by! Psalm 119:1 says,
"Blessed are the undefiled in the way, who walk in the law of the

Lord." That which is undefiled is clean and perfect, without blemish and upright. Our behavior will set us apart and it most likely will not be with the majority!

Young Christian women should strive to be Christ-like. By humbly submitting ourselves to obediently "walk in the law of the Lord," our lives will reflect an authenticity and trust-worthiness. His Words will supply us with wisdom, and His presence will be an endless source of assurance and support.

Weed #4: Weed of Insincerity

Characteristics: Likes to dwell in the shade, appears healthy but is susceptible to disease.

Caution! What you see with this one, is not what you get! Do not transplant!

Cure? Soil needs tilling on a regular basis; rake to a fine, smooth texture.

1. What words did Paul use in Philippians 1:10 to describe the condition of the believer at the time of Christ's coming?

    _____

2. Our English word **sincere** comes from the Latin words *sine* (without) and *cera* (wax). During the heating/cooling process of pottery-making, a jar could suffer minor cracks. Melted wax would be used to patch the flaw and keep the piece intact. A flawless vessel would be *sine cera* (without wax). How can hypocrisy in your life prevent you from being useful in the Lord's service?

    _____

    _____

    _____

3. A potter could usually pass off a defective piece as flawless, unless it was held up to the sunlight. Only then would the item be revealed as what it truly was. The Greek word used for sincere is *eilikrines*, which means "judged by sunlight." God's glorious light of perfection will always reveal our inadequacies. How genuine have you been when "judged by sunlight"?

_____

*Try not to have a "cracked pot" testimony when held up to God's expectations of righteousness!

4. In James 5:12b, it is stated, "but let your yea be yea; and your nay, nay". Even though James is referring to oath-swearing and promise-making, how would this statement apply to someone who wants to show sincerity?

_____

_____

5. Unexpected circumstances, areas of temptation, and the pressure to conform frequently test our faith. Our testimony is most at stake when we are "under fire." God's Word has given us many examples that show the weak side of man (and woman!). Look up the following passages and record your observations.

	Who is the hypocrite?	What was taking place?	Action or Result
Luke 22:57–62			

	Who is the hypocrite?	What was taking place?	Action or Result
Acts 5:1–11			
Matthew 26:14–16			

6. In contrast, the Bible has many role models who exemplified an unfaltering, extraordinary trust despite the adversities and afflictions.

	Who is being spoken about?	Words describing them	Action or Result
Genesis 7:1			

	Who is being spoken about?	Words describing them	Action or Result
Job 1:8			
1 Peter 2:21–23			

7. Most importantly, it is our responses that reveal the most about us. What instruction does Matthew 5:44 give?

_____

_____

_____

8. Finally, meditate on 1 Samuel 12:24. How can this verse keep your walk with the Lord accountable and sincere?

_____

_____

_____

Weed #5: Weed of Deception

Characteristics: Attractive and fragrant, yet oozing with acidic, artificial tendencies.

Caution! Will make a repeated attempt to grow back--cannot overlook this nuisance!

Cure? Full, direct sunlight should eliminate its threat.

1. What synonyms do the following verses use for deception?

   ~ Genesis 3:13 _____

   ~ Psalm 34:13 _____

2. Deceiving someone has the implication of being premeditated, that is, "a deliberate choice to lead someone in a false way." Where do you think this state of mind arises from?

   _____

3. What does God's instruction in 1 Samuel 16:7 reveal to Samuel about the true character of man?

   _____

   The heart is the most interior organ in your body. The Scriptures use the heart figuratively to refer to one's feelings, will, and/or intellect. Determine which term (feelings, will, or intellect) each reference below uses:

   ~ Exodus 4:21 _____

   ~ Psalm 73:21 _____

   ~ Romans 10:9 _____

4. What is one of the best things you can use your heart for? (See Psalm 119:11, 15, and 48.)

_____

5. What phrase describes the sinner's condition in Isaiah 29:13?

_____

6. If we're allowing God's Word to sink in deep (to the heart), it will be more difficult to contradict that character when tested. Compare Psalm 119:32 to Proverbs 12:20a. What else will naturally take place if your heart is receptive to God's precious promises?

_____

7. God looks for what kind of heart in us when we have sinned and chosen to be deceptive? (See 2 Chronicles 34:27.)

_____

8. **Just for fun,** see how many adjectives you can find in the Bible that describe the heart of a sincere believer in Christ.

_____

Weed #6: Weed of Judging Others

Characteristics: Spacious and non-selective in its environment; camouflages well.

Caution! Most varieties tend to be frost-resistant! Thrives in moist climates.

Cure? Crop rotation is a must; replenish with mulch and rich nutrients.

1. Christ's perfect insight, as revealed to us in Scriptures, is remarkable, isn't it? He spoke with compassion, with authority, and without hesitation. The parables He taught were vivid illustrations that imparted wisdom and understanding to His listeners. And, it is interesting to see divine revelation taking place in the hearts of those He singled out! In Luke 7:38–50, the sin of judging others is so clearly depicted. Read it carefully and then answer the following questions.

   ~ Look at verse 39 again. Who is judging whom? _____

   _____

   ~ What did the woman do to show her sincerity? _____

   _____

   _____

   ~ What did the host and others with Jesus do to show their sincerity?

   _____

   ~ Who is Jesus addressing in verse 40? _____

   ~ Note that in verses 39 and 49, the Pharisee and those at the dinner are guilty of harboring judgment, but how is it expressed?

   _____

2. What do you think is taking place in the heart of an individual who sheds tears?

   _____

3. Can someone guilty of judging others also possess a spirit of humility?

   _____

4. What can be done to bring about a change of heart in a teen that constantly struggles with the sin of hypocrisy?

   _____

   Look up these verses and write down what emotion(s) triggers tears of humility.

   ~ Psalm 119:136 _____

   ~ Psalm 120:1–2 _____

   ~ John 11:35 _____

   ~ 2 Corinthians 2:4 _____

   ~ Acts 20:19 _____

5. Read the passage of Matthew 7:1–5, which addresses the topic of judging others falsely.

   ~ Have you ever had someone say "Don't judge me!"? _____

   ~ What kind of an attitude is revealed by this comment?

   _____

   ~ Do you think this behavior is frequently expressed? _____

   Why? _____

6. Often, the imperfections we see in others are actually something we may be personally struggling with. It certainly explains why we are so overly-sensitive and quick to pass judgment on others! This tendency to magnify another's flaw while diminishing our own is hypocrisy. What objects are used in this passage that describe the issues . . .

In ourselves? _____

In others? _____

7. Why do you think the object in our eye is described as the larger item?

_____

_____

_____

8. Refer to Matthew 7:5. What necessary action must be taken in our lives before we attempt to help someone else?

_____

_____

_____

9. Matthew 7:7–8 follows up this controversial subject with a beautiful promise that we can claim in times of need. If hypocrisy is a weed that you want to keep out of your spiritual garden, what traits would you want to ask, seek, and knock for?

_____

_____

_____

10. It's important that our conduct with other believers is not injurious to the cause of Christ. Romans 14:13 reminds us of the significance of promoting peace with other believers. Write it out below.

_____

_____

_____

Did this section on judging others make you reconsider how you behave toward others? Pray and ask God to help you be more sensitive and caring. Here is a list of questions to ask yourself the next time you are tempted to speak out in judgment:

• Am I in a critical state of mind?

• Am I truly concerned about (fill-in-the-blank)'s action/attitude?

• Am I guilty of the same thing I am judging in the other person?

• Am I willing to address the issue(s) in my life so that I am not a hypocrite?

• Am I trying to make myself look good or better by speaking out in judgment?

• Am I causing this person to sin because of my harsh conduct?

• Am I willing to pray for this person?

• Am I willing to help this person?

• Am I committed to respond like Christ does no matter what?

Digging Deeper—seeds of sincerity

Has your spirit been one reflecting criticism, hypocrisy, or dishonesty? It might be time to check your motives and discern the intent of your heart. Does it please Christ to know what unspoken judgments are inside of you? Let's not use hypocrisy as a cover-up or a solution. We may fool those around us, but God sees the inner workings of our hearts.

Hypocrisy is a weed which commonly springs up year round. Make sure its symptoms aren't creeping into your spiritual garden!

Peter reminds us in 1 Peter 2:1–2 to lay aside "…all malice and all guile and hypocrisies…," and to "…desire the sincere milk of the word that ye may grow thereby." The remedy to avoiding insincerity is to fill the inner being of yourself with the only pure nourishment that can sustain and mature you. Pray like the psalmist did in Psalm 69:5, and rely on God's power and cleansing to make you a useful vessel of His excellence. Write this prayer out below and commit it to memory today.

_____

_____

_____

Weeding your Garden

Purity

> Dear Diary, Andy, the softball coach, is awesome! He drives a new Camaro and lets me ride shot-gun to all the games! Tonight, after practice, he offered to take me home. We stopped first at his house but no one was home. I really didn't feel very comfortable there, but he is soooo gorgeous, and he likes ME!

Hmmm…what's wrong with this diary entry? I remember how flattering it was to have the notice of a good-looking and athletic guy! (Did I mention he was rich too?!) I was sixteen years old and very naïve. I hadn't really given any thought about the compromising situation Andy had placed me in.

Although nothing happened—physically speaking—I had seriously let my guard down. Comparing one's purity to a fortress, mine was in a much weakened state. A few more excursions with Andy and who knows what strongholds would remain! In this instance, I had let emotions overrule and dictate my actions, allowing an opening for temptation to possibly sneak in.

The weeds which can choke the virtue of a young Christian lady are subtle. They creep in unnoticed, blending in, becoming part of the growth process. After a while it is hard to distinguish them from the healthy, original specimen. What could have been a flourishing

and productive product now is spoiled and suffocated by an abundance of harmful influences and weak morals.

Girls, we have to remember that we are in a battle! If Satan destroys your reputation because of an impure relationship, then he has rendered you ineffective *and* defective. We can NOT lose our salvation, but a marred testimony carries guilt and misery with it. Our objective has to be focused on pleasing God, who has commanded us to "be ye holy; for I am holy" (1 Peter 1:16).

Weed #7: Weed of Immodesty

Characteristics: Bold, colorful, and luscious appearance; instantly recognizable.

Caution! Yields destruction and undermines crop productivity!

Cure? Carefully select your sources and develop a well-laid garden plan.

1. When we hear the word *modest*, we usually think of the outward appearance and a standard that it represents. The word *modest* can be found in 1 Timothy 2:9. What is being described as modest?

   _____

   ~ Can one wear appropriate clothing, but still be considered immodest? Explain your answer.

   _____

   _____

   _____

   _____

2. What additional qualities are mentioned in 1 Timothy 2:9–10 that godly women should adorn themselves with?

   _____

~ What kind of an attitude is shown in a woman who follows this counsel?

_____

_____

_____

~ If we maintain a mindset that encourages these behaviors in our daily lives, do you think modesty is an attainable goal?

_____

3. Strong's Concordance defines the Greek word *kosmos* (for modest) as something which has been placed in an orderly arrangement or in proper order. Our English word *cosmos*, which symbolizes the heavens and/or the universe, is derived from *kosmos*. Think of the deliberation and careful detail that God utilized when He created our world! Immodesty would be contrary to the character of a holy God, who desires order and accuracy. Would displaying the actions or attitudes of immodesty please God?

_____

~ Do you think modesty should be a priority in the life of a godly teen girl? Why/why not?

_____

_____

_____

_____

_____

4. Modesty could be described as: one's desire to appear well in the sight of others. Complete the chart, noting how this quality was displayed.

	Who is being described?	How are they being described?
Esther 2:7, 15		
1 Samuel 25:3		
Proverbs 31:10–31		
Acts 9:36		

5. In the previous references, it is not mentioned whether these women dressed modestly or immodestly; it seemingly is their moral character that makes an impression! What we display on the exterior should reveal what is on the interior. We aren't just focusing on being modest in a physical sense anymore, but in a spiritual sense.

   ~ List attributes which could characterize both the inner and outer qualities of a modesty-centered testimony:

   _____

   _____

   _____

   ~ Purity can only be characterized by holy living. If others were to describe your outer appearance, would it mirror what is inside of you?

   _____

6. Revelation 21:2 describes the new holy city, Jerusalem, "prepared as a bride adorned for her husband." What images come to mind when you imagine the appearance of a bride in a wedding ceremony?

   _____

   ~ **Adorned** is a counterpart to **modest**, taken from the same Greek root word, portraying something which has been decorated. What are servants instructed to adorn themselves with in Titus 2:10?

   _____

7. Taking this illustration of adorning a step further, what is described as an ornament in 1 Peter 3:4?

    _____

    ~   How does God feel about this type of character? _____

    _____

8. The ornament of a meek and quiet spirit is a wonderful thing to put on! Strong's Concordance translates the action to "put on" as "sinking into a garment." We might not actually clothe ourselves in this manner, but such imagery reminds us that we should be completely covered with what we put on! That's modesty to the max! This theme of adorning ourselves or "putting on" is stressed multiple times in the Scriptures. Note the attributes that we can acquire by following the instruction to put on.

    ~   Romans 13:12 _____

    ~   Ephesians 6:11 _____

    ~   Colossians 3:10 _____

    ~   Colossians 3:12–14 _____

    _____

9. Reflect on this statement: Holiness is a characteristic unique to God's nature that becomes the goal for human moral character. Has holiness been a garment that you put on daily? How can having such a character trait help you maintain a modest appearance?

    _____

Weed #8: Weed of Impurity

Characteristics: Usually a hybrid (mix) specimen; of a poor quality.

Caution! Foliage from this unwelcome garden guest is unattractive and unclean!

Cure? Thoroughly irrigate entire garden site and drain well.

1. Read 1 Corinthians 6:19–20. How is your body described?

   _____

2. The Greek word used for temple in this passage is the same one that signifies "a sacred place"—the same word used throughout the Bible meaning "a sanctuary." What other synonyms could describe such a place?

   _____

   ~ A spiritual temple is dedicated to holiness. What command is given in verse 20?

   _____

   ~ It is stated in this reference that our bodies and our spirits are not our own. What two reasons explain this statement?

   _____

   _____

   _____

   (For more information on this topic, please see Chapter 10.)

3. We honor God when we take proper care of our bodies! According to Genesis 1:27, how were man and woman created?

   _____

~ No other created being can claim that distinction! Identify some of the ways in which you can take good care of your body.

_____

_____

4. Taking improper care of your body and disrespecting its sacredness is sin. Purity relates to every aspect of our lives: how we think, talk and behave. Purity pleases God and shows Him a life sold out to obedience. In the chart below, list the activities or attitudes that can be distinguished as pure or impure:

Pure in Heart/Mind:	Impure in Heart/Mind:
Pure in Language:	Impure in Language:
Pure in Body:	Impure in Body:

5. Sanctified is to be "declared clean and holy." What does 1 Thessalonians 4:3–4 state about sanctification?

    ~   What specific sin are we advised to abstain from?

    ~   What does 1 Corinthians 6:18 say about this particular sin?

    ~   What additional sins are listed in Ephesians 5:3–4 that reveal impure conduct?

6. What motivation is given in 1 Peter 1:15–16 for us to live holy lives?

    ~   Becoming holy is a continuous process. Refer to 2 Corinthians 7:1 and identify the right response to this calling.

7. As we take the necessary steps to work toward this goal, God gives us hope and encouragement. How is His Word described in Proverbs 30:5, Psalm 12:6 and Psalm 119:140?

8. What does Psalm 119:9–11 claim that God's Word can do for us?

_____

9. Read Galatians 5:16–17. What instruction is given?

_____

~ How does obeying this order help us remain pure?

_____

_____

_____

~ What constant battle do believers repeatedly face?

_____

~ Sin cannot reign where purity has taken up residence! An impure lifestyle, whether it is in the flesh or in the spirit, is in direct contradiction to what God desires of us.

10. God uses the word *upright* to portray someone who is without blemish, perfect, and complete. What is considered upright in the eyes of the Lord in Psalm 119:137?

_____

Read these verses and record the benefits of being upright:

~ Proverbs 28:10 _____

~ Psalm 37:37_____

~ Psalm 84:11 _____

11. In addition, God's Word will guide us and give us wisdom. Look up James 3:17, and list the qualities of the wisdom that comes from above.

_____

_____

~   Are you willing to commit today to seek this wisdom and be obedient to God's command to be holy?

_____

Weed #9: Weed of Impatience

Characteristics: Rapid growth; maintains a very short cultivation season.

Caution! Act fast with this one! Remove all signs of vegetation without delay!

Cure? Transfer healthy seedlings, which remain unaffected, into individual clay containers.

1. I think one of the most difficult "weeds" for a teen girl to keep out of her spiritual garden is the weed of impatience. Its presence wreaks havoc, stirring up irritability and unnecessary pressure. Impatience can be defined as "the inability to control one's desire for action."

Do you consider yourself a patient person? _____

Why/Why not? _____

~   What are some "things" a young woman has to wait for?

_____

_____

~ How can impatience be a bad influence, especially when it comes to staying physically pure?

_____

_____

~ Although what we wait upon may be a good thing, our desire to rush a particular event or decision can have devastating consequences. List what results can occur.

Physically: _____

Emotionally: _____

Spiritually: _____

2. What counsel is given in Proverbs 4:23, concerning our affections?

_____

~ The choices we make originate from the heart. Refer to 1 John 2:16 and identify the worldly temptations which confront all of us.

_____

~ Can the sins of lust and pride cause an impatient attitude?

_____

Explain: _____

_____

_____

_____

3. As a result of being impatient, we can rush God's plan. One example is given in Genesis 16: 1–4 of an individual who did not wait. Explain the circumstances.

_____

_____

~ Was God still faithful to fulfill His promise spoken in Genesis 15:4–5?

_____

~ How? (See Genesis 21:1–3.) _____

_____

4. An incredible illustration of patience is given in the account of Jacob and Rachel (Genesis 29:16–30). How much time did Jacob spend serving Laban in order to acquire Rachel as his wife?

_____

_____

_____

~ Would it have been God's Will for Jacob to be impatient? ____

5. Look up the following three references and complete the statements.

~ Romans 15:5—He is a God of _____

~ Romans 15:13—He is a God of _____

~ Romans 15:33—He is a God of _____

~ How would these assurances help a teen who is struggling with the decision to be patient?

_____

_____

_____

6. What are some of the blessings we receive when we "wait on the Lord"?

~ Isaiah 40:31 _____

~ Psalm 40:1 _____

~ James 1:4 _____

7. How can Ecclesiastes 3:11 help us to be content with our present circumstances?

_____

_____

_____

8. What phrase does the psalmist repeat four times in Psalm 13:1–2?

_____

~ Is it the cry of one who is patient or impatient?

_____

~ Is it the plea of one who is strong or weary? _____

_____

9. Being impatient will certainly wear us down! It's important that we grab onto God for all the gusto we need! God uses the "waiting times" in our lives to refresh and renew us.

~ Record what Isaiah 40:28 states about God's stamina.

_____

~ What directive does the psalmist give in Psalm 27:14?

_____

~ When we feel powerless, what does Isaiah 40:29 say we can count on?

_____

10. God's power and presence will supply peace—something quite needful when impatience is on the horizon! As you write out Isaiah 26:3 below, make a commitment to trust Him fully in every situation, whether it's sooner … or … later.

_____

_____

Digging Deeper—Seeds of Purity

It will take incredible power and determination to remain modest, pure, and patient.

Compare yourself to a clay pot which encloses a vulnerable sapling. Okay, that sounds a bit strange … but you get the picture, right? Our purity must be guarded and guarded well.

You are probably familiar with this quote from Proverbs 31:10, "Who can find a virtuous woman? For her price is far above rubies." Rubies are the rarest of all the gemstones. They are known for their hardness, durability, luster, and uncommonness. Consider this: *your purity* is more valuable than a precious jewel stone!

Purity is not only a choice, but it is a command and a long-lasting commitment. You must have a **battle plan** ready and know what response is right and God-honoring. Stay focused on making purity a priority and you will exemplify the finer qualities of a virtuous woman!

Here are a few suggestions:

- Scripture Memory is key! Search the Word for the assurance you need and claim it personally!

- Learn to recognize the Holy Spirit's promptings. He is real! If you feel in your heart/soul that it's wrong—it probably is!

- Meditate on God's Word daily—His Word is the "Sword of the Spirit" (Ephesians 6:17). Use it to defend yourself from Satan's attacks on your purity!

Other ideas:

- Ask for prayer support.

- If you're struggling with certain temptations, go to your parents or a trusted adult! Having accountability with a godly peer can also be an asset.

- Re-evaluate your motives and goals periodically—write them down, and check where you are! Your walk with the Lord should always be going forward, not backwards! If you feel distant from Him, draw closer, and He will draw nearer to you—that's a promise in James 4:8! How to draw closer? Read more, pray more, ask more, and thus, expect more.

NOTE: Perhaps this section convicted you of unwise choices concerning how you dress or behave. Have you failed to be patient and pure, participating in activities that are destructive to your body and spirit, not considering the consequences? Have the lusts of the flesh and eyes caused you to be sexually promiscuous? God does not put these limits on us to keep us from having fun or to ruin our lives. Sex is reserved for marriage-it's all a part of His plan for you; He wants the affections of your heart and His Will is your sanctification. If you have been physically impure, please do not feel useless and abandoned. Satan loves to discourage us, by filling our minds with doubt and despair. God has a wonderful plan for your life; you can make a fresh commitment today to remain pure in heart, language and body. Get alone with God, confess the sin(s) of impurity you have been involved in, and ask for His forgiveness. God will forgive and strengthen you as you determine to do right! With God's help, you can begin anew.

> Psalm 51:2 says, "Wash me thoroughly from mine iniquity, and cleanse me from my sin."

We have a God Who is willing to meet us where we are. Once we have vowed to honor Him with our minds and body, we can expect great things! And we won't regret it!

Sowing a Peaceful Presence

Tame your tongue

Mary was a girl who lived in our neighborhood. She wasn't very attractive, but was a bit overweight and clumsy. Boys were annoyed by her and most of the girls kept their distance. "Moo-Moo" was the taunting nickname labeled upon her—to the extent that people eventually forgot her real name!

Numerous times I reflect back on my upbringing. I was raised in the city, so there was a certain hardness that I acquired as a result of being street-smart savvy. Name-calling, teasing, spreading false information, and telling "little white lies" were a daily dose of the language system that I used to communicate with friends and family.

James 3:5 tells us that "the tongue is a little member and boasteth great things. Behold how great a matter a little fire kindleth." Once a spark begins to smolder, it doesn't take long for it to develop into a raging blaze. It can set us on a course of destruction, leaving behind a trail of hurt and desolation. Yet the same fire that possesses the ability to maim can be the warmth we seek when chilled to the bone. Under different circumstances, its intensity and constancy can be a balm which restores and refreshes our weary souls. Our speech carries the same powerful energy.

Remember the childhood chant, "Sticks and stones may break my bones, but names will never hurt me"? That's not true. Names *do*

hurt. And so do the false innuendos, the cover-ups, and the negative and critical comments. We need to choose our words carefully and realize we cannot control or reverse the damage they can do.

Weed #10: Weed of Dishonesty

Characteristics: Beautiful, robust, and award-winning potential; lacks substance.

Caution! Found in all habitats—greenhouse (sheltered) or garden (open-air)!

Cure? Sandy, dry soil should prevent its spread; keep shearing tools in close proximity.

1. What commands are given in the following verses concerning our speech?

    ~   Psalm 34:13 _____

    ~   Proverbs 4:24 _____

2. Proverbs 12:22a states that "Lying lips are abomination unto the Lord." An abomination is that which is disgusting and hated. How can knowing the holy character of God help deter us from habitual lying?

    _____

    _____

    _____

    _____

3. What explanation is given in Ephesians 4:25 for why we should not lie?

    _____

4. According to Colossians 3:9–10, why should we avoid dishonesty?

_____

_____

5. The knowledge being spoken about in Colossians 3:10 can be translated as "full discernment" or "being fully acquainted with." Where can we find this type of knowledge or discernment?

_____

6. What does the psalmist hate in Psalm 119:163? _____

~ What does he love? _____

7. Another reason to not be associated with lying can be found in John 8:44. Who is being spoken about concerning dishonesty?

_____

~ The originator of a custom in Biblical times was often re-ferred to as the "father" of that practice. Which family tradi-tion—lies or truth—would you rather follow?

_____

8. Spiritual warfare is something we probably don't think about much, but it does exist! Satan's tactics of trickery and contradiction are ageless. Do you recall how he deceived Eve in the Garden of Eden? According to Revelation 12:9, who has the Devil succeeded in deceiving?

_____

9. Ephesians 6:11–17 describes the protective devices needed to combat our adversary. What part of our spiritual armor is to be equipped with truth?

_____

10. The girdle was designed to keep every part of a soldier's armor in place. How can knowing the truth of God's Word (the Bible) establish stability in your life?

_____

_____

11. According to Psalm 119: 29–30, what choice can we make that will help us overcome the sin of dishonesty?

_____

Weed #11: Weed of Gossip

Characteristics: Edible, juicy and flavorful; possesses a strong after-taste.

Caution! Exposure to this wild flower is dangerous to one's health!

Cure? Avoid direct contact; when necessary, saturate the source of its origination.

1. What comes to your mind when you hear the word "gossip"?

_____

2. What kind of words will we be responsible to give an account of in the day of judgment in Matthew 12:36?

_____

3. Gossip can be defined as idle or useless talk. In 1 Timothy 5:13, what kind of behavior results from one being idle?

_____

4. What term is used in these verses describing someone who spreads information?

   ~ Proverbs 16:28 _____

   ~ 2 Thessalonians 3:11 _____

5. What damage is done by a talebearer's (or gossip's) words in Proverbs 18:8 and Proverbs 26:22?

_____

6. How trustworthy is an individual who spreads information (see Proverbs 17:9 and 20:19)?

_____

7. Read Psalm 86:15 and write the qualities of God that are acknowledged.

_____

   ~ Which traits are especially abundant? _____

8. *Mercy* and *truth* are also paired together and mentioned in these passages. Identify what good things come about when mercy and truth are ever-present.

   ~ Psalm 25:10 _____

   ~ Psalm 61:7 _____

   ~ Proverbs 16:6 _____

9. How could possessing these characteristics (qualities listed) help us control the temptation to gossip?

    _____

    _____

    _____

10. In ancient Biblical days, thick stone walls were built around the circumference of a city. The watchman, positioned atop the walls twenty-four/seven, was responsible for warning the gatekeeper of any imminent danger. A friend could easily gain access. Yet, if an enemy was sighted, the entrance into the city would be impassable. The request in Psalm 141:3 to "Set a watch, O Lord, before my mouth; keep the door of my lips" illustrates this concept of careful discernment when it comes to our speech. Our lips are like the gate into the city, allowing friend or foe—truth or trash—to pass its entranceway! Refer to John 14:16–17 and John 16:13.

    Who acts as our watchman? _____

11. One more point to consider, God is omnipresent—always with us! He knows every word we utter! Write out Psalm 139:4 below and meditate on its significance and accountability.

    _____

    _____

    _____

Weed #12: Weed of Negativity

Characteristics: Blooms rarely; covered with barbed needles, found in dark shady patches.

Caution! Don't let this creeper fool you! Its clusters are hardy and impressive!

Cure? Heavy doses of kindness, optimism and joy are required to eradicate its influence.

Satan has an agenda—namely, to displace God's position of authority and righteousness in our lives. When we sin with our tongue, we have "given place to the devil" (Ephesians 4:27). In other words, his influence is crowding out a Holy God. In addition to dishonesty and gossip, our talk can reflect other forms of negativity.

1. In the following passages, identify other wrong uses of the tongue.

    ~ Proverbs 7:21 _____

    ~ Psalm 15:3 _____

    ~ Psalm 22:7 _____

    ~ Psalm 12:3 _____

    ~ Hosea 4:2a _____

2. In the Bible, God often uses "word pictures" to illustrate close associations between unlike objects. Look up the verses and identify what item the tongue is compared to.

    ~ Psalm 52:2 _____

    ~ Isaiah 30:27 _____

    ~ Psalm 64:3 _____

    ~ Jeremiah 9:8 _____

3. Name the deadly substance likened to the tongue in Psalm 140:3, Romans 3:13, and James 3:8.

_____

4. What type of harm can be inflicted on one who is on the receiving end of such dangerous tools or substances?

_____

5. Proverbs 18:21 and James 3:10 give two striking contrasts concerning the purpose and power of our speech. What are they?

_____

6. When was the last time you blessed the Lord with what you said? What comes out of our mouths should honor God. Write out some of the right uses of the tongue.

   ~ Psalm 40:5, 10 _____

   _____

   ~ Psalm 63:3-5 _____

   ~ Psalm 96:2 _____

   ~ Psalm 107:1 _____

7. How aware are you of the impression you make with your words? Read Acts 16:19–34 to discover of one of the most powerful, evangelistic events that took place—in a prison nonetheless! What was so unique about Paul and Silas' verbal conduct?

_____

_____

8. What events resulted from their contagious joy and positive witness? (See verses 31–34.)

   _____

   _____

9. Match up the circumstances of Paul and Silas with James' words in James 5:13. What kind of relationship did they obviously have with God?

   _____

   _____

10. How can having a close relationship with God help us control our tongue?

   _____

   _____

Digging Deeper—Seeds of Peace

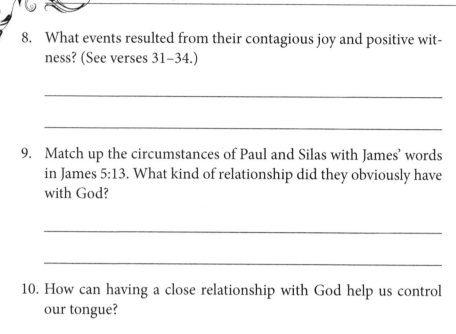

Did the topic of an untamable tongue strike a nerve? Our excuses for loose lips, critical comments, and false facts will fall flat before an omniscient (all-knowing) and omnipresent Savior. Developing restraint with *what* we say depends on developing the recognition for *why* we say it!

When we sow a peaceful presence, weeds like negativity, gossip, and dishonesty will rarely take root. An imbalance in our character—namely the positive traits outweighing all else—is actually okay! God's presence is synonymous with peace. The Scriptures claim innumerable times that He is the "God of peace"!

Ephesians 4:29 states, "Let no corrupt communication proceed out of your mouth but that which is good to the use of edifying." Worthless words and useless conversation are not constructive. The Greek definition for edify can be interpreted as "to be a house-

builder." Think of your speech as a form of architecture that has the power to produce a magnificent mansion or reduce it to rubble! Which structure would you rather create?

Write out Colossians 3:16. _____

_____

_____

_____

Are You a Crowd Pleaser?

Peer Pressure

Summertime . . . new friends . . . hanging out on the Hill
. . . . . . it's nice to feel like I fit in . . . I don't have to do
everything they do . . . . . . I can just say "no" . . . or can I?

What happened next? My initial response of a firm "no" soon became a hesitant "maybe," then finally, a meek "yes." It took time, but the constant exposure to activities of this group wore me down, and I eventually yielded. It's the classic pattern of peer pressure. And the teen years are ripe for its influence and manipulation.

The persuasion is strong, nearly over-powering, preying upon those who seek approval and acceptance. Rising up against it is not usually the popular choice. It's easier to go with the flow, not make any waves, tolerate the demands, and meet the expectations.

What is the consequence to this progressive and far-reaching force that misrepresents a true friendship? Usually a bad reputation will result from involvement with the wrong crowd. Proverbs 22:1 says, "A good name is rather to be chosen than great riches." To be well spoken of is of great value, but it is a choice <u>we</u> make.

Yet, why does peer pressure have to suggest such negative or wrongful interactions? Numerous times in the Scriptures the word *brethren* is used, which identifies a close association of believers.

Being a part of God's family enables us to obtain innumerable brothers and sisters in Christ! We can find freedom and stability with those who share the same personal relationship with our Heavenly Father. And the encouragement and knowledge we gain will strengthen us to stand apart with confidence!

Weed #13: Weed of Insecurity (lack of confidence)

Characteristics: Shy, somewhat retreating species; blends in well with ground cover.

Caution! Cuttings from this character can wreak havoc and weaken arrangements!

Cure? Easily uprooted; generous applications of assuredness will foster a finer product.

1. Having friends and hanging out is not a bad thing. What does Psalm 133:1 say about brethren who dwell together?

   _____

   ~   How should they dwell? _____

2. God wants us to have a unified spirit in our relationships. What word is used in Philippians 2:2 that describes this oneness?

   _____

3. Read 1 Corinthians 1:10. Paul gives instruction to the brethren to be "perfectly joined together". How?

   _____

   _____

4. The *mind* indicates intellect and knowledge while *judgment* refers to opinions. Why do you think God stresses unity and similarity in our relationships? (See Romans 12:16, 2 Corinthians 13:11, and 1 Peter 3:8.)

_____

_____

_____

5. Security develops from the solid trust one has in another. According to Psalm 118:8, who should we trust?

_____

~ What else can we trust in (Psalm 119:42)? _____

6. In Psalms 135:15–18, what do the heathen trust in? _____

~ How are they described? _____

_____

_____

7. Is it possible to have security in someone or something we do not trust?

_____

~ Could insecurity then be labeled as mistrust? _____

8. While in prison, Paul wrote a letter to the church at Colosse (Colossians 1:2). How does he address the members?

_____

_____

_____

~ In verses 3–6, Paul details the positive characteristics of this group (which he had never met!). How many can you find?

_____

_____

_____

~ What did this knowledge motivate Paul to do (verse 9)?

_____

_____

9. Read Colossians 1:21–23. What had taken place at one time?

_____

God restored the Gentiles from a life of bad choices, sin and idolatry—probably insecurity too! He can do the same for you!

10. Write the words used in verse 23 that speak of confidence and steadfastness.

_____

~ If you have trusted Christ as your firm foundation and source of security, write three to five sentences, explaining how this happened in your life.

_____

_____

_____

_____

_____

Weed #14: Weed of Apathy (lack of interest)

Characteristics: Dull, droopy leaves; most commonly found in isolated, barren regions.

Caution! Displays manipulative tendencies and will pose a threat to healthy shrubs!

Cure? Major overhaul is in order; start anew with fresh, vitamin-rich loam.

1. To understand what apathy is, one needs to understand what apathy is not. What word in 2 Kings 10:16 describes the desire one has for the Lord?

   _____

2. Taken from the Greek word *zeo*, zeal literally means "to be hot" or "to boil". You've heard the expression "on fire for God"? That's describing an intense enthusiasm, a deep-rooted interest in pleasing and serving the Lord. In the following passages, write out what is being desired or sought after.

   ~ Nehemiah 1:11 _____

   ~ Job 31:35 _____

   ~ Mark 11:24 _____

   ~ 1 Corinthians 14:1 _____

   ~ 1 Peter 2:2 _____

3. Not having a passion (for something or someone) creates indifference, a lack of motivation and subsequently, a sense of isolation. And that's when we are most vulnerable! Read Ephesians 2:10. What is our purpose to fulfill?

   _____

4. Does exhibiting apathy work for or against this purpose? Why?

_____

_____

_____

_____

5. How does having an apathetic attitude affect our choice of friends and activities?

_____

_____

_____

_____

6. Look up the following verses and indicate if the peer pressure exerted would be a positive or negative one.

~ Ephesians 4:32 _____

~ Psalm 55:14 _____

~ Proverbs 23:20 _____

~ John 3:20 _____

~ Ephesians 5:11 _____

~ Proverbs 27:6 _____

7. God wants us to show evidence on the outside of what has taken place on the inside. If we have trusted His Son for our eternal security, there is no reason to be passive and silent with what we know! Note what kind of attitude is expressed.

    ~ Psalm 27:6 _____

    ~ Psalm 18:48-49 _____

    ~ Romans 10:15 _____

    ~ 1 Peter 2:9 _____

    ~ Would these responses be considered positive or negative?

    _____

8. God's Word needs to be a vital part of our life. With it, we can expect God to fulfill His promises and provide for our every need; without it, we are lost, without direction and hope. Write out 2 Timothy 3:16–17, which beautifully details its intended purpose.

    _____

    _____

    _____

9. Apathy will not only weaken our reverence for God's Holy Word but will also weaken our appreciation for its presence. After Jesus' resurrection, His followers mourned the loss of their master/ teacher/friend (Luke 24:15–35). Little did they realize that His presence could be found in the Scriptures!

    ~ What effect did the stranger's words have on the two who conversed with him by the way (verse 32)?

    _____

    _____

~ How could this example stir up zeal for God's Word in your life?

_____

_____

10. The Greek word used for "quicken" is the same word used for "revive." Both verbs suggest action: acceleration and restoration. Who has enabled the psalmist to be revived in Psalm 85:6 and Psalm 138:7?

_____

~ What other source can cause quickening? (Refer to Psalm 119:25, 50, 107 and 154.)

_____

11. When we submit to God and take an interest in His Word, then our souls will naturally respond with action and that should decelerate the apathy! Look up the following verses and record what results from knowing His Word.

~ Psalm 119:52 _____

~ Psalm 119:133 _____

~ Jeremiah 15:4 _____

~ John 6:68 _____

~ Romans 15:4 _____

12. **Just for fun**, read Psalm 119 and see how many synonyms you can find for God's Word.

_____

_____

Weed #15: Weed of Ignorance (lack of knowledge)

Characteristics: Independent, distinct markings; requires little care.

Caution! Seeds are tiny and can turn up anywhere!

Cure? Restore garden bed with diligence and abundance of prayer.

1. Refer to James 1:5 and answer the following:

   ~ When we lack wisdom, who can we count on to supply it in abundance?

   _____

   ~ Write out the definition for upbraid.

   _____

   ~ Do we ever have to hesitate or doubt that God will supply us with the knowledge we need? Why or why not?

   _____

   _____

   _____

   _____

   _____

   ~ What promise is also found in this verse? _____

   _____

2. Read Proverbs 24:5 and Ecclesiastes 7:19. What can wisdom do for us?

   _____

   _____

3. After referring to Proverbs 24:10, complete the following word analogy.

    _____ wisdom/ _____ strength

    _____ wisdom/ _____ strength

4. How do you think strength/wisdom ties in with resisting (negative) peer pressure?

    _____

    _____

    _____

5. Wisdom from God also helps us deal with temptation the Biblical way. In the account of Jesus' fasting and temptation in the desert (Luke 4:1–13), what does Jesus use to contest Satan's challenges and contradictions?

    _____

6. It helps to memorize Bible verses and apply them when we are tempted to "follow the crowd." Explain how the following verses could be a help.

    ~   Psalm 1:1–2 _____

        _____

    ~   Philippians 4:13 _____

        _____

    ~   1 Peter 4:14 _____

        _____

        _____

7. What aspects of our lives are influenced by the presence of God's Holy Spirit?

   ~ John 16:13–14 _____

   ~ Romans 8:26–27 _____

   ~ 1 Corinthians 2:12–13 _____

   ~ Galatians 5:22–23 _____

   ~ 1 John 3:24 _____

   _____

8. As Solomon is beginning his reign in 2 Chronicles 1:7-12, God is willing to grant Solomon whatever he requests. What is Solomon's reply in verse 10?

   _____

   ~ What additional benefits are given because of Solomon's choice?

   _____

   _____

   ~ How long of a reign did the Lord allow ?(See verse 30.) _____

   _____

9. What evidence of these blessings are given in 2 Chronicles 9:22–23?

   _____

   _____

10. To be wise, one must be willing to be taught. Psalm 25:5a cries out to God, "Lead me in thy truth and teach me." What attitude is essential as well?

   _____

11. Pray for God to help you cultivate a mind-set of meekness, and a desire to grow in wisdom! Write out Psalm 119:66.

_____

_____

_____

Digging Deeper—Seeds of Strength

Remember Superman? Although famous for his super-human strength, Superman had a weakness: kryptonite. Just one tiny fragment could render him weak and inactive! The "man of steel" had no hope of regaining his physical might unless the rock was removed from his presence as soon as possible.

In contrast, spiritual strength draws upon an endless reserve of divine mineral! There is no limit to its capabilities or consequences. Deuteronomy 32:4 states, "He is the Rock, His work is perfect; for all His ways are judgment." We can <u>always</u> trust God to provide us with energy and discernment.

Negative peer pressure is a foe we must confront. A firm foundation in Christ assures us victory, despite the odds and despite the oppositions we face. To overcome insecurity, we must claim the Father as our source of confidence; to overcome apathy, we must claim the Word as our source of motivation; to overcome ignorance, we must claim the Holy Spirit as our source of wisdom. Only then can our testimony be one that brings glory to Him!

What Comes Out of You When You're Squeezed?

Having the right responses

Flashback: I'm 15 years old and my mother, who has just had major abdominal surgery, is depending on me to help with meals, housework, and babysitting during her recovery.

My reaction? Not good. Instead of recognizing the experience as an opportunity to show my dependability, I complained about all the fun I was missing out on. And, to make matters worse....*gulp*... I wrote a letter to my mother expressing those bitter feelings!

I didn't realize that my attitude was the by-product of a high pressure situation, (a.k.a. stress!). My social life, my personal life, my (fill-in-the-blank) life, was being squeezed with inconveniences and demands *not* chosen by me. And what came out of me was sour juice! A positive, cooperative response would have honored my parents and pleased the Lord. My negativity showed a spirit that lacked the sweetness of a Christ-centered testimony.

An anonymous quote, "When we think right, there is always an abundance" is written in my Bible, next to Philippians 4:17: "Not because I desire a gift: but I desire fruit that may abound to your account." Paul's words to the Philippians were stressing the importance of a visible testimony. If our actions and attitudes—our fruit—

line up with God's Word, others will see the evidence. "Thinking right" means there may be some nasty weeds to pull. Removing bad attitudes that have taken up residence in our hearts is necessary so that we can make room for the nourishment we need.

Weed #16: Weed of Complaining

Characteristics: Fine, threadlike fibers completely cover its trunk and branches.

Caution! It's best to discover this one early! Has the uncanny ability to rub off on others!

Cure? Dust frequently with doses of enthusiasm and delightfulness.

1. Look up Philippians 2:14–15. What responses are we commanded not to have?

    _____

    ~   Under what circumstances? _____

    ~   What reasons are given for this command? _____

    _____

    _____

2. God's Word mentions several areas which can be affected by our choosing to behave unpredictably and unpleasantly. Identify where a complaining or unwilling spirit has already set in or has the potential to.

    ~   Luke 10:40–41 _____

    ~   1 Peter 4:9 _____

    ~   2 Corinthians 9:7 _____

3. The account of the Israelites' deliverance and journey to the Promised Land of Canaan is referenced in 1 Corinthians 10:10–11. Why did this experience occur, and why is it significant to us?

   _____

   ~ Why would God want to warn us about such behavior?

   _____

4. What is it that the Israelites are unhappy about in the following passages?

   ~ Exodus 16:1–3 _____

   _____

   ~ Exodus 17:1–3 _____

   _____

   _____

5. Moses follows God's instruction to send a representative from each tribe to explore the land of Canaan (Numbers 13:1–3). In verses 25–33, the men return to report on their findings. Once again, the people find occasion to grumble! Refer to Numbers 14:1–4 and record their responses.

   _____

   _____

   _____

6. Not everyone was a naysayer! Read Numbers 14:24 to find out what was different about the response of Caleb. What two reasons are given?

   1. _____

   2. _____

~ Who else does God say will inherit the Promised Land in Numbers 14:30?

_____

_____

7. What is the consequence for the children of Israel? (See Numbers 14:29–34.)

_____

_____

_____

~ Why would this wrong attitude cause God's judgment to prevail?

_____

_____

_____

~ How are we like the Israelites when it comes to responding to pressure and change?

_____

_____

8. Our problems and worries can certainly prevent us from trusting Jesus' Words. David states in Psalm 119:92, "Unless thy law had been my delights, I should then have perished in mine affliction." How often do you turn to the Scriptures for enjoyment and encouragement?

_____

9. In John 16:33, the expression "but be of good cheer" is used by Jesus as He addresses His disciples. Jesus was preparing His followers for the time when He would no longer be present with them. What has God given us in return?

    _____

    ~   Jesus punctuates the same verse with this statement: "I have overcome the world." What do these words assure us of?

    _____

10. What instruction is given in Philippians 4:4 and 1 Thessalonians 5:16 that can surely bring "good cheer"?

    _____

    ~   What do you think is required of us in order to conquer a complaining attitude?

    _____

    _____

11. List the promises you can find in John 15:16 that will give you victory over a grumbling spirit.

_____

_____

_____

_____

Weed #17: Weed of an Angry Spirit

Characteristics: Has a high tolerance to extreme temperatures; roots run deep into ground.

Caution! Harsh, hard-edged leaves will NOT easily break free!

Cure? Must be sheltered from other vegetation; Allow it to wither in seclusion.

1. Ephesians 4:26a gives the instruction to, "Be ye angry," yet it includes a restriction, "and sin not." How can one display anger and not sin in their actions, thoughts, or deeds?

_____

_____

_____

_____

~ Look at the latter part of Ephesians 4:26. How would you write this out in your own words?

_____

~ According to Ephesians 4:27, who are we pleasing when we display an angry spirit?

_____

2. Wrath is defined as lasting anger. There may be situations in which anger is justified; however, if not dealt with properly, it becomes a long-term liability! Observe in Genesis 4:4–8 how Cain's envy quickly escalates into a deadly outcome. In verse 5, what is stated about Cain's attitude when his offering is presented to the Lord?

_____

_____

3. In verses 6 and 7, the Lord questions Cain's reaction, and states the effect of good choices (if one does well) versus bad choices (if one does not do well). What happens when we make a bad choice?

    _____

    _____

    _____

4. Due to the lasting anger that Cain would not relinquish, what ultimately happened? (See verse 8.)

    _____

    _____

    _____

    ~   What other emotions can fester as a result of anger being stirred up within us?

        _____

    ~   Are we able to control an angry spirit in our own strength?

        _____

5. What additional warnings concerning anger are given in Psalm 37:8?

    _____

    ~   How do you think this is possible?

        _____

        _____

        _____

        _____

6. The book of Proverbs provides us with much insight regarding our relationships with others. Look up the following passages and fill in the blanks below.

   ~ Proverbs 14:29—One exhibits _____ when they are slow to anger.

   ~ Proverbs 16:32—Controlling your anger requires _____.

   ~ Proverbs 29:22—Anger stirs up _____.

   ~ Proverbs 25:23—Anger can affect our _____.

7. What measures are given in James 1:19–20 that would help deter someone from displaying outbursts of anger?

   _____

   ~ What is the best way to prevent a situation from becoming more fierce and fiery (Proverbs 15:1)?

   _____

8. There's an adage that states, "A believer at war with his brother cannot be at peace with his (Heavenly) Father." Hebrews 12:14 and Romans 12:18 stress the importance of maintaining peace with others. The Greek interpretation for peace is to "set at one again," implying a joint, harmonious bond. Keeping this definition in mind, explain why God places such a high priority on the attribute of peace.

   _____

   _____

   _____

   _____

   _____

9. Having an angry-free testimony will bless God first and fore-most. When all else around us seems to be falling apart, we can have confidence knowing that God is the One in charge, and He is not in a panic about any of it! How is God described in 1 Cor-inthians 14:33?

_____

~ God's very essence is one of serenity and stillness—the exact opposite of anger!

10. How could you be ready to withstand the temptation to sin with an angry response?

_____

_____

_____

_____

Remember this! The greatest remedy for anger is delay!

Weed #18: Weed of Discouragement

Characteristics: Easily known by its droopy, weak framework; lacks motivation.

Caution! Very twisted foliage—notorious for its stubborn, entangled clasp.

Cure? Metal fencing or caging recommended for a firmer support system.

1. Hannah was discouraged. She was barren, constantly being reminded of that fact by Peninnah, who had many children. Look up 1 Samuel 1:10. What action did Hannah seek in order to overcome her bitterness?

_____

2. A situation that troubles us will trigger a reaction. Read the following passages to discover what was done when dismay set in.

   ~ Psalm 119:71 _____

   ~ Job 1:20 _____

   ~ Matthew 8:23–25 _____

   ~ Luke 8:43-44 _____

     _____

   ~ 1 Peter 5:7 _____

     _____

3. The Scriptures are full of promises of peace, strength, and hope. The definition of hope is "a feeling that what one desires will happen." How can an attitude of hope help combat discouragement?

   _____

   _____

   _____

   _____

4. What can result in one who does not have hope? (See Proverbs 13:12.)

   _____

   ~ On the other hand, what will occur if we *do* have hope (Psalm 31:24)?

     _____

5. What does Psalm 73:26 declare will eventually fail us?

_____

~ How would Philippians 4:13 help someone who is discouraged?

_____

_____

_____

~ What quality mentioned in Psalm 27:14 is also required for those who will be strengthened by God?

_____

6. Titus 2:13 puts a greater perspective on what we can hope for. What are we told to anticipate?

_____

~ Are you behaving in a way that reflects anticipation of the Lord's coming?

_____

7. What two words describe God in Psalm 71:5?

_____

8. God's Word is rich with the assurance of hope! As you read Psalm 31, note the extreme range of emotions and the despair David had. In verse 14, what does David declare?

_____

9. In Psalm 31:24, what will occur from having hope in the Lord?

_____

10. What does God say about "His ways" in Isaiah 55:8-9?

_____

~ How can trusting "His ways" in **every** situation help us reflect the godly attribute of an encouraging spirit?

_____

Digging Deeper—Seeds of Sweetness:

When you are squeezed, what comes out of you? Are you quick to complain, or do you lash out in anger? Perhaps a discouraged heart dictates your mood the majority of the time. An irritable nature is difficult to control, whether it is ours or another's!

It's our sin nature that causes us to react wrongly. Sin blocks our communion with a Holy God, who sees all and knows all. Unless the barrier is eliminated, our ability to overcome any onset of disturbances is destined to fall short and fail utterly.

Isn't it reassuring to know that we have a merciful, patient God who is able and willing to forgive us when we respond inappropriately? Let us bravely forsake the grumbling, let go of the resentments and focus on that which is positive and uplifting.

One of the Bible's most steadfast promises can be found in 1 John 1:9. Confess the sin that has kept you in bondage, and restore your relationship with God today! Write it here.

_____

_____

_____

Bloom Where You Are Planted!

Contentment

> Dottie was an only child who lived across the street from me. Dottie's grandmother was raising her and gave her anything she wanted. Although Dottie would brag about her "stuff," she never seemed truly happy. She looked mad most of the time, hardly ever smiling. What was her problem!?!

Have you encountered someone like a "Dottie" in your life? If so, she probably made an impression on you—a bad one! Discontentment is a slick cover-up for someone who harbors an ungrateful heart and a lack of security. Its irritating effects are infectious, spreading anxiety, disregard, and mischief, like… a weed!

What Dottie lacked was the assurance of God's love in her life. 1 John 4:19 declares, "We love Him because He first loved us." Oh, the comfort she could have experienced from knowing that God loves her and is patiently waiting, ready to listen and forgive. Dottie probably needed stability too. One's "stuff" is just a temporary fix for a void that can only be occupied by a personal relationship with Christ. This familiar quote from Hebrews 13:8, "Jesus Christ the same yesterday, and today, and forever," testifies of the firm, never-changing foundation found in Christ and Christ alone.

Proverbs 3:26a promises, "For the Lord shall be thy confidence and shall keep thy foot from being taken." The pessimistic outlook that Dottie had, could have been corrected with the knowledge of God's promises. A hopeful heart is a happy heart!

Letting go of what disheartens us is no easy task, but we have someone who is all-sufficient to bear our burdens and gives us strength to endure. God's plans for us are perfect and personal. With God on our side, we can claim victory in those problem areas that cause discontentment!

Weed #19: Weed of Fear (Lack of trust)

Characteristics: Feeble yet fast-growing; prefers the shade and less-trodden paths.

Caution! Just one little sprout can do serious harm; be attentive to its influence.

Cure? Cover with a jam jar and press down well into soil— predators will pass over.

1. When we use the word fear in this section, it is descriptive of one who is in a state of apprehension. Often, we display this characteristic when we are "out of our comfort zone," meaning we are venturing into an unknown situation.

    ~ Describe a time when you may have felt out of your comfort zone:

    _____

    ~ What two-worded command is spoken by God in Genesis 26:24, Judges 6:23 and Isaiah 41:14?

    _____

    ~ What reason is given in Psalm 118:6 for why we should not have fear?

    _____

2. Lacking trust in what God can do, in ANY situation, is like saying to God, "You can't have control of this—not yet anyway!". It will affect our attitude and the way we present ourselves. What do the following verses say about trusting God?

~ Psalm 5:11 _____

~ Psalm 71:5 _____

~ Isaiah 26:4 _____

~ Proverbs 29:25 _____

3. How does Psalm 62:8 describe God? _____

~ How often should we trust in Him? _____

4. Trust requires consciously letting go of our fear(s), and leaning upon that which will support us. What are we advised not to lean upon in Proverbs 3:5–6?

_____

5. What are the three elements of the spirit that God gives us in 2 Timothy 1:7?

_____

6. Let's examine the consequences for someone who trusted God and utilized the spirit of God's power in 2 Chronicles 14:1–11. After his father's death, Asa took over as king of Judah. How does Asa honor and please God in this role (verses 2–5)?

_____

~ What results from Judah's obedience (see verses 6–7)?

_____

_____

~ Seriously outnumbered by the Ethiopians, Judah will have to take action and go to battle. What is Asa's first response (verse 11)?

_____

~ Does Asa's prayer sound like a man who is fearful or lacking trust?

_____

~ What happens in verses 12–15? _____

_____

_____

~ How difficult is it for you to have trust in God's power when facing an overwhelming or intimidating situation?

_____

7. God's loving spirit is always with us. According to Romans 8:38–39, what can separate us from the love of God?

_____

8. Refer to 1 John 4:9–10 and John 3:16. Explain how God's love for us was ultimately shown.

_____

_____

~ Is there a time in your life when you recognized your need for God's love?

_____

9. Write out 1 John 4:18. _____

_____

_____

~ Why is there no reason to fear with the love God gives us?

_____

_____

10. With the help of the Holy Spirit and the knowledge that God's Word gives us, we can reap blessings of peace and protection. However, it takes discipline to maintain the spirit of a sound mind. Read Philippians 4:6–9 and answer the following questions.

~ If we heed the instruction in verse 6, what are we assured of in verse 7?

_____

_____

_____

_____

~ According to verse 8, what things should fill our minds?

_____

_____

_____

~ Who will be with us, if we practice and put into action what we have seen, heard, and learned (verse 9)?

_____

Weed #20: Weed of Doubt (Lack of faith)

Characteristics: Needs a generous amount of space (soil) and attention (watering).

Caution! Wide range of varieties, perseveres in almost all climates!

Cure? Aggressive, and thorough treatment required—no doubt about it!

Remember Eeyore, the downcast donkey-friend of Winnie-the-Pooh? His troubles weren't nearly as terrible as he thought. His brooding on the uncertainties of his dilemma soon became the key issue instead! We all can be like Eeyore when it comes to facing future circumstances, can't we? Dwelling on disbelief and dismay, we become convinced of sure failure—before the battle has begun. No need to fear! Faith will bring trust, which will conquer fear and doubt.

1. Read Jeremiah 29:11. What kind of thoughts does God have towards us?

   _____

   ~ What is it that the Lord desires to give us?

   _____

2. Strong's Concordance reveals a deeper interpretation for us: *expected* symbolizes hope, the "thing that I long for", and *end* translates as "a happy issue." God's intentions for us are always good and positive. What additional words in Psalm 139:17–18 describe the thoughts of God?

   _____

   ~ Is it God's Will for us to be content? _____

   ~ Whose choice is it to be discontent? _____

3. What instruction is given in James 1:6 and Mark 11:24 concerning prayer?

_____

_____

~ Is this suggestive of one who is strong or weak in the Lord?

_____

4. The most accurate definition of faith is found in Hebrews 11:1. Write it out below.

_____

_____

5. Refer to Romans 8:25, to see what should naturally accompany our expectancy.

_____

6. What kind of faith is described in these passages?

~ Deuteronomy 32:20 _____

~ Matthew 8:10 _____

~ Luke 12:28 _____

~ Colossians 1:23 _____

7. It's been said that "Faith is like a muscle, and prayer is the exercise that helps it grow." We can conclude then, that with much prayer, there is much faith, right? What can alleviate doubt?

_____

~ Are you one who gives *much* time to *much* prayer?

_____

~ Would you rate your faith as little or much?

_____

~ How would you rate your tendency to doubt?

_____

8. According to Romans 10:17, where does faith come from?

_____

~ Sitting under the preaching of God's Word and prayer are essential for a faith-centered life. In Hebrews 12:2a, what does it tell us about Jesus' association with our faith?

_____

~ Knowing this principle, should we have any doubts about our future?

_____

9. What three-word phrase in Luke 11:13 and Luke 12:28 implies that the kindness bestowed on us from our Heavenly Father is beyond compare?

_____

10. If we are to claim a testimony of contentment, how should we handle the times when we are tempted to doubt? (See Hebrews 11:6.)

_____

_____

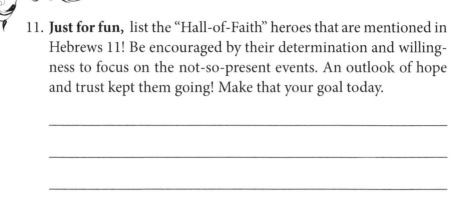

11. **Just for fun,** list the "Hall-of-Faith" heroes that are mentioned in Hebrews 11! Be encouraged by their determination and willingness to focus on the not-so-present events. An outlook of hope and trust kept them going! Make that your goal today.

_____

_____

_____

_____

Weed #21: Weed of Ingratitude (Lack of appreciation)

Characteristics: Very independent; tends to isolate itself from other garden varieties.

Caution! Springs up in the most unexpected places!

Cure? Nurture with TLC; add considerable portions of warmth and gratefulness.

☺☺☺ . . . ℳakes me recall a story I once read. An elderly couple had a custom of drawing the happy-face icon on small note cards with the letters "*SHMILY*" printed underneath. They would tuck their cards in various places (i.e. a sock drawer, a closet shelf, etc.), expecting the other to eventually discover it. The acrostic "**See How Much I Love You**" was an encouraging reminder of the warmth and happiness that still existed—after sixty years of marriage!

I like to think that God has placed SHMILY signs all around us too! His presence is manifested in the answers to prayer, the beauty of creation, and the fellowship we have with other believers—just to name a few! How frequently do you thank Him for what He has given you? Our state of contentment is directly proportional to the measure of appreciation we reciprocate. When we become discontent with our circumstances, we have failed to recognize God's goodness and blessings.

1. Perhaps one of the best illustrations of a thankful spirit is given in Luke 17:11–18. Jesus, on His way to Jerusalem, encounters ten lepers, who cry out to Him for healing. What does Jesus command them to do in verse 14?

   _____

   ~ How do the lepers initially respond?

   _____

   ~ What happens in verses 15–16?

   _____

   _____

   ~ What does this example teach us?

   _____

   _____

2. The book of Psalms is an ideal place to go when searching for Scripture that is praiseworthy and honoring to God. Read the verses and notice what attribute is being recognized with praise, thanksgiving, and a happy heart!

   ~ Psalm 21:13 _____

   ~ Psalm 28:7 _____

   ~ Psalm 35:9, Psalm 40:16 _____

   ~ Psalm 118:24 _____

   ~ Psalm 139:14 _____

3. What sense of generosity does God express to His children in Matthew 7:11?

   _____

4. What are we instructed to not forget in Psalm 103:2?

_____

~ According to Psalm 68:19, how often can we expect them?

_____

5. Refer to 1 Thessalonians 5:16–18 to find the three commands that are given.

_____

_____

_____

~ Write out the last part of verse 18. _____

_____

~ Did you know that you are in God's Will when you obey instruction from His Word to rejoice, pray, and give thanks?

6. What do you think is our biggest obstacle when it comes to being ungrateful?

_____

_____

~ What mind-related action in Deuteronomy 8:18, 1 Chronicles 16:12, and Psalm 77:11 can help us to be aware of God's goodness?

_____

~ What are some ways whereby one could display this frame of mind?

_____

_____

~ Do you keep a journal of answered prayer requests?

_____

It would be a great resource to refer to when discontent starts to nag your thoughts!

7. What are the blessings of a merry heart in Proverbs 15:13 and 17:22?

_____

_____

_____

8. There is a source of delight that is always nearby—see if you can find it in Psalm 16:11.

_____

~ What else can we get from being in His holy company? (See 1 Chronicles 16:27.)

_____

9. Whether it is mercies or miseries we receive from the hand of our Heavenly Father, we must not overlook the occasion to give thanks. Make it your mission to prioritize thankfulness! Write out Colossians 3:17.

_____

_____

_____

Digging Deeper—Seeds of Satisfaction:

A seed will not sprout until it is placed in the ground where it will almost immediately respond to warmth and moisture. Similarly, our spirits remain dry and dormant until nurtured by the presence of faith and hope. Once we become aware of God's presence and promises in our lives, thankfulness should naturally follow. What a glorious specimen!

Jeremiah's words of prophesy in Jeremiah 32:41, "I will rejoice over them to do them good…and I will plant them in this land assuredly with my whole heart and my whole *soul*." Where has God "planted" you? Have you expressed a response that shows maturity and acceptance? God is the Masterful Gardener who has firmly placed you where He knows you will be nourished and supplied with all that is needful. Verse 42 continues with reassurance: "…so will I bring upon them all the good that I have promised them." Have you responded to His loving care for you with total trust, unfailing faith, and active appreciation?

Contentment requires action on our part! Let us remember His Word, rich with the assurance of rest and security. Let us praise the One Who has power to remove the fears and doubts that afflict us. And let us bloom where we are planted, declaring as the psalmist did in Psalm 136:1, "O give thanks unto the Lord; for He is good: for His mercy endureth forever."

Withering or Weathering?

Wrong Influences

> My Uncle George's attic was a great hiding place,
> especially once I discovered the stacks of abandoned
> romantic novels stored there! I would indulge myself
> for hours on end, reading page after page of their
> seductive, racy contents.

Many times we *know* that the activities that fill up our time are not right. Yet, we participate in them anyway, foolishly justifying our sin. My interest in reading wasn't wrong, but the material I chose was! Why else would I seek out such a private location? Our "hiding places" are actually a frail disguise for the secret, selfish pleasures we possess.

We live in a ME-centered generation, where pop culture seems to set the precedence. Sources of entertainment such as music, media, movies, and television subtly manipulate our thinking and behavior. Their portrayal of the latest fads and fashions dictates our choices and influences our etiquette. In due time, the ability to distinguish right from wrong begins to lessen, numbing our sensitivity to God's standards. A once vibrant testimony withers into a sad state of waywardness and abandonment.

How do we address the onslaught of wrong influences? Jesus frequently advised his audiences: "He that hath ears to hear, let him hear" (Matthew 11:15, Luke 8:8). In other words, the highest attention should be given to what has been spoken! Taking heed to its

instruction will give us both firmness and insight, plus increase our awareness of what lies ahead.

Weed #22: Weed of Disobedience

Characteristics: Extremely damaging, vine-like creeper grows enthusiastically in clusters.

Caution! Every gardener has to deal with this one—stay vigilant!

Cure? Destroy diseased plants at once; leave no traces of its residue!

1. Disobedience and obedience have this in common: they are both a deliberate act of the will. How is sin defined in James 4:17?

   _____

   ~ Is choosing to disobey a sin? _____

2. When we commit sin, what does John 8:34 say we have done?

   _____

3. Making a choice—whom or what you will serve—requires a commitment. Read Romans 6:16 to get an idea of how this decision becomes secured. Answer the following:

   ~ What are the two options one has? _____

   _____

   ~ Who is your master when you choose to sin? _____

   ~ Who is your master if you choose righteousness? _____

   Matthew Henry's Concise Commentary expresses the master/ servant association this way: "Christ never will own those who yield themselves up to be the servants of sin." Have you realized that giving into sin jeopardizes what you have, *or could have had,* with Christ?

4. According to Isaiah 59:2 and Psalm 66:18, how does the presence of sin affect our relationship with God?

_____

5. God takes sin seriously! It is in direct opposition to His holy nature. What does Paul cite as "contrary" in Galatians 5:17?

_____

~ What descriptions are used in Romans 8:5–8 for those who are concerned with earthly things?

_____

~ What does verse 8 assert that they are unable to do?

_____

6. Galatians 5:19–21 lists the works (deeds/acts) of the flesh; while verses 22–23 of the same chapter identify the fruit of the Spirit. Write them in below.

~ WRONG influences:

_____

_____

_____

_____

_____

~ RIGHT influences:

_____

_____

_____

_____

_____

7. Observe the developments that occur in Matthew 13:22 and Mark 4:19 when one follows the world's enticements and traps. What ultimately happens?

_____

8. How should we respond to a wrong influence? (See Ephesians 5:11.)

_____

_____

~ The action of reproving here means "to convince them that they are wrong." What is necessary in order to get that point across?

_____

_____

~ Read John 3:20 and explain what happens when our evil deeds are brought into the light.

_____

~ Would a teen who is living an obedient lifestyle have to be ashamed of his/her deeds being exposed?

_____

9. Our defense strategy must include God's Word. Learn to trust it as your . . .

~ source of _____ Psalm 119:104

~ source of _____ Psalm 119:143

~ source of _____ Psalm 119:9

~ source of _____ Luke 4:32

~ source of _____ Hebrews 4:12

10. What kind of influence can a Christian teen have in the world?

   ~ Matthew 5:13 _____

   _____

   ~ Mark 1:17 _____

   ~ Ephesians 5:8, Philippians 2:15 _____

   _____

11. Choosing obedience over disobedience will surely win out! As you write out Psalm 119:101, make a fresh promise to remain obedient.

   _____

Weed #23: Weed of Foolishness

Characteristics: Young, immature specimen; seedlings are a real nuisance.

Caution! Only experienced care-takers can identify this wacky weed!

Cure? No fooling around with this one--remove at first signs of growth.

1. Those who misuse wisdom are regarded as being foolish. In the following passages, specify what characterizes a fool:

   ~ Psalm 14:1 _____

   ~ Proverbs 1:7 _____

   ~ Proverbs 15:7 _____

   ~ Proverbs 18:6–7 _____

   _____

2. What does Proverbs 28:26 tell us that a fool trusts in?

_____

~ What instruction is given in Proverbs 3:7?_____

_____

~ Explain how relying on "self" alone can affect the decisions you make.

_____

_____

3. What kind of activity is associated with a fool in Proverbs 10:23?

_____

~ Compare that with a fool's conduct in Proverbs 14:9. How is sin viewed?

_____

4. Both 1 Corinthians 1:18 and Ecclesiastes 2:14 give us insight as to why the foolish display such negative qualities and opinions. What are the consequences for someone who has rejected the truth and wisdom offered by God?

_____

5. Throughout God's Word, light represents knowledge and truth, while darkness is symbolic of ignorance and foolishness. What does the light described in 2 Corinthians 4:6 reveal?

_____

~ Why would mankind choose the darkness rather than the light (John 3:19)?

_____

_____

6. What promise is stated in John 8:12?

   _____

   _____

   ~ Have you allowed this promise to guide you into a loving, right relationship with Jesus Christ?

      _____

7. Read Ecclesiastes 2:26 and write down the three things that God gives to those who please Him.

   _____

   ~ What word in Proverbs 3:13 describes the man who finds wisdom and understanding?

      _____

   ~ Refer to Psalm 119:104 to find where this source of knowledge comes from.

      _____

   ~ Who else is involved with providing us with this wisdom and revelation of knowledge (Ephesians 1:17)?

      _____

8. What does Proverbs 9:10 say about wisdom and knowledge?

   _____

   _____

9. What must one do in order to have understanding?

   ~ Job 28:28 _____

   ~ Psalm 111:10 _____

10. Once we acknowledge our dependence on the Lord, the understanding we gain from His wisdom ought to be put into action. Applying it to our everyday experiences is the <u>real</u> test!

   ~ Personalize Psalm 37:31 by writing it out, substituting your name in place of the pronoun *his*.

   _____

   _____

   _____

Weed #24: Weed of Poor Discernment

Characteristics: Weak quality; blends naturally with surrounding shrubbery.

Caution! Crowded beds and rows are inviting company for pest and disease attack!

Cure? Keep soil fertile with frequent watering; add nutrients on a daily basis.

1. When it comes to making decisions, the weed of poor discernment can be a headstrong rival, forcing us to compromise or choose wrongly. Read 1 Kings 3:5–9 and describe what is happening.

   _____

   _____

   _____

2. Why would Solomon make this specific request? _____

   _____

   _____

3. Discernment literally means to discover! Obviously, poor discernment will lead us to make wrong choices. But an understanding heart, as Solomon so eloquently states, will always prove beneficial. Quote the expressions that are used in the following passages which plead for God's affirmation or direction.

    ~   Psalm 27:11 _____

    ~   Psalm 105:4 _____

    ~   Psalm 143:8 _____

        _____

4. When we draw close to God by studying His truths, we will become "in tune" with His desires for us. What feelings are experienced by the author in Psalm 40:8 and Psalm 119:35 regarding God's Will and Word?

    _____

    _____

    ~   How does Proverbs 18:2 describe someone who does not have these emotions?

        _____

5. Psalm 1:2 takes this idea of seeking pleasure in the Lord's Law a step further. What else accompanies this yearning?

    _____

    _____

    ~   Do you strive to meet with the Lord daily? Is it with an attitude of expectancy and enjoyment, or is it a dutiful act of drudgery?

        _____

6. Our spiritual walk can be so much richer once we have grasped the magnitude of God's endless resources! Find the numerous promises given in Proverbs 2:6–8 that support this statement.

_____

_____

_____

7. It's been said that there is only an eighteen-inch difference between "head" knowledge and "heart" knowledge. Obviously that is referring to a physical location, but the heart knowledge is deep-rooted—it will bear evidence of fruit in your Christian walk.

~ How can the promises mentioned in Proverbs 2:6–8 help a teen who is facing tough choices?

_____

_____

_____

_____

8. According to Proverbs 2:9-10, what kind of effect does this knowledge have on an individual?

_____

~ Where must wisdom reside? _____

9. What are the actions of those in Proverbs 2:12–19 who remain opposed to God's Way of righteousness?

_____

_____

_____

_____

10. Does Proverbs 2:20–21 describe someone who has wise or poor discernment?

_____

~   What measures could you take to maintain a testimony that reflects wise discernment?

_____

_____

_____

Digging Deeper—Seeds of Wisdom:

It may be time to review and/or renew your position in Christ. Have wrong influences wilted your dependence upon the Lord? Have you habitually chosen to disobey, discount, or disguise sin in your life? Only the authority of God's Wisdom can help us withstand the worldly pressures and persuasions. Knowledge, understanding, and discernment are the by-products of a wise, God-centered soul. Here are some recommendations for a victorious result:

- **Relinquish the hiding places!** Jeremiah 23:24 proclaims: "Can any hide himself in secret places that I shall not see him? . . . Do not I fill heaven and earth? saith the LORD."

- **Repent of the secret sins!** Psalm 90:8 states: "Thou hast set our iniquities before thee, our secret sins in the light of thy countenance."

- **Reach for more resources!** Romans 11:33a exclaims: "O the depth of the riches both of the wisdom and knowledge of God!"

- **Restore (bring back) the joy!** Psalm 51:12 requests: "Restore unto me the joy of thy salvation; and uphold me with thy free spirit."

Taming the Terrain

Authority Issues

After high school, I went on to further my education. As a dorm student the first year, I enjoyed the freedom and fun that came with living on campus. I lived at home the second year, under the rule of my parents once again. Their meddling and control over my life really got on my nerves!

Life became rather rocky on the home front. Not only did I disobey the instated curfew rules that were imposed upon me, but my heart was hard and disrespectful towards my parents. My rationalization for such conduct was: "I'm an adult; I don't need *them* to tell *me* what to do anymore!" I wanted to live by my terms, and I made sure that message was evident!

Why didn't I realize I was causing such disappointment and heartache around me? The maliciousness that accompanied my rebellious spirit was neither partial nor practical in its selection. It just seeped in like a poison, tainting everything it touched. My determination to esteem self—*and only self*—as the authority was even blasphemous to God!

Preventative measures must be in place to avoid the pitfalls and penalties that <u>will</u> occur from an unyielding spirit. Heed the command to be attentive in Hebrews 12:15: "Looking diligently lest (in case) any man fail of the grace of God; lest (in case) any root of bitterness springing up trouble you, and thereby many be defiled." Yes,

a sense of firmness is needed; however, it is with the fixed assurance of trusting God supremely. Subjection to our authorities will naturally follow once our dependence is wholly upon Him.

Weed #25: Weed of Bitterness

Characteristics: Unmistakable, pungent aroma; deep, far-reaching roots.

Caution! Thrives remarkably well in dry, barren soils!

Cure? Apply liberal mix of gentleness and goodness to stifle its erratic growth.

1. We all experience disappointment. Whether it's an unmet expectation or a friend who has let us down, we have to be careful that our emotions do not escalate into anger or resentment. Bitterness is a sinful response to an injustice or perceived injustice. Describe a time when you know you harbored feelings of bitterness.

   _____

   ~ Were you able to overcome this incident? If so, how?

   _____

2. Perhaps you have heard the axiom: "Be bitter or be better." Life's lessons can be teachable moments or critical calamities! God's Word gives us numerous examples of those who dealt with hostility or unfair treatment. The life of Joseph is one that could have had disastrous consequences had he reacted differently. In Genesis 37:3, as we see his account unfolding, what two reasons are given that explain the animosity of his brothers?

   _____

   ~ What additional information is stated in verse 4 that shows a progression of this emotion?

   _____

~ What kind of reaction is brought about in verses 5–11?

_____

_____

3. What events take place in verses 12–24?

_____

_____

_____

_____

~ The brothers decide to spare Joseph's life and sell him to a passing caravan instead. What other sins are committed by Joseph's brothers? (See verses 31–35.)

_____

_____

_____

_____

4. Joseph is sold into slavery, and excels in his position as a slave to Potiphar, an officer of Pharaoh's. What do Genesis 39:3, 21, and 23 affirm about Joseph's character?

_____

_____

~ What does this imply about Joseph's relationship with God?

_____

~ Do you think Joseph's testimony helped prevent bitterness from setting in?

_____

5. While serving in Potiphar's house, Joseph is falsely accused of an immoral act and consequently imprisoned for it. Through it all, Joseph remains steadfast in his faith, trusting God. How different and difficult the outcome would have been if Joseph had chosen to be bitter!

    ~ Name the authorities that were in Joseph's life.

    _____

    _____

    _____

6. Because Joseph remained sensitive to God's leading and timing and was in subjection to his authorities, the lineage of Christ was preserved. Joseph's act of forgiveness and restoration with his brothers typifies the Divine Will of our Heavenly Father. It was Divine intervention that saved the people of Israel and Divine intervention that sent the Son to be the propitiation (substitute) for the sins of the whole world (1 John 2:2).

    ~ Write out Genesis 50:20.

    _____

    _____

    _____

7. Refer to the following passages and complete the questions:

	Who is speaking or being spoken about?	What is their response to an authority?
Exodus 5:2		

	Who is speaking or being spoken about?	What is their response to an authority?
Ruth 1:16		
Matthew 8:8–9		
Luke 2:42–48, 51		

8. What happens when bitterness finds a place to dwell? (See Ephesians 4:31.)

_____

_____

~ How is this reflected in Genesis 27:41?

_____

_____

_____

~ Due to the tense, bitter relationship that existed between them, Jacob and Esau parted ways. However, the brothers were reunited....twenty years later! Describe the scene found in Genesis 33:1–4.

_____

_____

~ How sad that it took such a lengthy time for Jacob and Esau to make amends! Is there anyone you need to make things right with or ask forgiveness of?

_____

9. What results, given in Philippians 1:12–14, helped Paul to focus on something other than bitterness while he was imprisoned?

_____

_____

_____

Weed #26: Weed of Pride

Characteristics: Showy, elaborate greenery that towers over surrounding vegetation.

Caution! Be on guard for this one—takes root just about anywhere!

Cure? Allow plenty of sunlight to minimize its spread; barriers (fencing, caging) are useful.

1. Pride symbolizes honor and pleasure—usually directed at self-achievement and personal accreditation. Whether we are the donor or the recipient of the attention given, we must be careful to attribute the praise and recognition to its correct source; otherwise, our intentions can reflect a shallowness and false superiority.

~ Use a thesaurus to find synonyms that describe this all-too-common weed.

_____

2. The Hebrew and Greek word commonly used for pride is interpreted as: "to be inflated with self-conceit." Obviously, this definition confirms the egotism, self-absorption, and insensitivity to others that are associated with an overconfident spirit. What also accompanies a proud heart ? (See Psalm 101:5 and Proverbs 21:4.)

_____

3. How can pride affect a teen's response to authority?

_____

_____

_____

_____

4. Refer to these verses to see what some of the consequences of pride are.

~ Proverbs 11:2 _____

~ Proverbs 16:18 _____

_____

~ Proverbs 28:25 _____

5. If we love God and fear (meaning respect/revere) Him, what does Proverbs 8:13 claim we should therefore "hate"?

_____

6. What word is used in Proverbs 16:5 to describe one who is proud in heart?

   _____

   ~ What else can appear prideful (Proverbs 6:17)?

   _____

7. What do James 4:6 and 1 Peter 5:5 claim about God's actions towards the proud?

   _____

   ~ Have you ever realized that God—known for His committed character of unconditional love and kindness—could choose to *not* respond to those who are caught up in this sinful mindset? What do these verses say about God's actions towards those who are humble?

   _____

8. The prognosis for a full-of-pride presence is poor and dismal. Yet, a meek heart finds favor with God and brings reward and recognition. Look up what is spoken by the following three individuals that shows a contradiction for self-acclamation:

   ~ In Genesis 41:16, Joseph's words:_____

   _____

   ~ In Matthew 3:11, John the Baptist says:_____

   _____

   ~ In 2 Corinthians 12:7, Paul declares: _____

   _____

9. Consider this statement: You can't glorify self and Christ at the same time.

   ~ Would you agree or disagree? _____

   ~ How often do you struggle with the concept of pride?

   _____

   ~ What actions can you do that would show you glorify Christ instead of self?

   _____

   _____

   _____

   Pride is a plant that doesn't grow well in the shadow of the cross.

Weed #27: Weed of Disrespect

Characteristics: Resilient and reckless in its environment; strong, offensive odor.

Caution! Gardeners beware—thorns, bristles, and sharp edges will cause injury!

Cure? Entire plant must be smothered and discarded for successful outcome.

1. List the individuals (or their occupations) who represent a form of authority in our lives. Identify their area of expertise.

   _____

   _____

   _____

   _____

2. Respect is defined: "to consider worthy of esteem or value." The Greeks literally translated it as "face-receiver"! How many times have you heard a parent or teacher command, "Look at me when I am speaking to you!"? Facing the one who demands our attention is a sign of respect. What word used in Proverbs 3:9 and Ephesians 6:2 would have a similar meaning?

    _____

3. Who or what are we instructed to honor/respect, in the following verses?

    ~   Deuteronomy 5:16 _____

    ~   Psalm 119:117 _____

    ~   1 Peter 2:17 _____

    ~   John 5:23 _____

4. Another interpretation of respect is "to regard with pleasure, favor or care"—conduct fitting for an obedient and agreeable spirit!

    ~   The character of Daniel (in the Old Testament) mirrored a life of reverence for a Holy, personal God. Notice some of the additional qualities that Daniel possessed.

What quality is seen or shown by Daniel?	Questions to ask concerning yourself:
	Do your friends and family members see an excellent spirit in you?

Daniel 6:3

	What quality is seen or shown by Daniel?	Questions to ask concerning yourself:
Daniel 6:4		Are you faithful and committed to things which pertain to God in your life?
Daniel 6:5:		Daniel's convictions were solid, based upon the firmness of God's law. Can others say this about you?
Daniel 6:16		The king realized that Daniel had a steadfast relationship with his God. Is your walk with God one that shows an attitude of strength and submissiveness?

5. What areas can be affected by the right kind of behavior?

~ Colossians 4:6 _____

~ 1 Corinthians 2:16 _____

~ Matthew 5:16 _____

6. A disrespectful response and attitude contradicts God's instruction to obey our authorities. What does Romans 7:19 state about this bent or tendency to choose wrongly?

_____

_____

7. We can rid ourselves of this pattern of wrongdoing by placing trust in God's divine wisdom, power and justice. What three positions are attributed to the Lord in Isaiah 33:22?

_____

8. Consult Daniel 2:21 to find out what God's role is when it comes to those who are over us.

_____

_____

~ How can recognizing God as our primary authority help us deal with other authorities that come into our lives?

_____

_____

_____

_____

9. Forsake disrespect! Rather, focus on the amazing assets of our Lord and Creator! Write out Revelations 4:11, thanking Him for the blessings and benefits that He abundantly provides.

_____

_____

_____

Digging deeper—Seeds of Submission

Have authority issues become a sore subject in your household? Are the growing pains of adolescence causing you to usurp the power that is not yours to possess? The biggest problem we deal with when it comes to submission is assigning to our egos VIP (very important person) status! To make matters worse: bitterness, pride and disrespect will quickly hitch a ride, when stubbornness and self-fulfillment are in the driver's seat!

Dealing with the authorities God has placed over us, requires a dutiful approach and an obliging temperament. Submission to authority was a quality that Christ exhibited and one that we should emulate. Philippians 2:8 sums it best, "And being found in fashion as a man, he humbled himself, and became obedient unto death, even the death of the cross." No finer example could be given that portrayed such true and unconditional surrender!

Taming the terrain means we need to be constantly enriching our souls with the resources of obedience and optimism. Unless we consistently remain sensitive to God's leading and timing, we will continually falter and/or fail in *all* areas that demand a submissive spirit. Once we acknowledge that God is *in* all and *above* all, our lives will generate a testimony of simplicity and satisfaction. What remarkable growth will take place!

The Perfect Fruit

Salvation

> July 8, 1987. Driving home from work on the 3 to 11 evening shift. The stars are brilliant tonight. I sense the presence of God looking down upon me. I feel very small and inadequate. Realizing my need, I cry out to God in prayer, knowing only He can save me from my sins.

I couldn't wait to get home and share the news with my husband! I felt such relief—months of struggling with accepting the truth, and now it all seemed to "click." Although I had many questions and still so much to learn, I knew in my heart that this decision was right. I was so sure of it.

I think the most precious promise in the Bible is stated in John 3:16, "For God so loved the world, that he gave his only begotten Son, that whosoever believeth in him should not perish, but have everlasting life." Remove the word *world* and insert a name—any name—and note the significance of the message:

> "For God so loved _____ that He gave His only begotten Son, that whosoever believeth in Him should not perish but have everlasting life."

God not only loves us unconditionally, but His character is one of generosity and grace: God "gave his only begotten Son." Would you be willing to give away something so valuable? I highly doubt

it! Salvation is often described as a "gift"—it requires nothing from us, except the action of receiving it. And once accepted, it is ours to keep!

Although the future is uncertain, it is reassuring to know that God's plans for us are purpose-driven, prayer-friendly, and power-supplied! Your testimony for Christ can be abundant with fruit—evidence that God's Holy Spirit has taken up residence in your heart. The weeds have been pulled, giving way to a fertile and promising site for new growth. The gift of salvation—knowing Jesus Christ personally as our Savior—*will* give us security and a deep-rooted faith to endure both the sunny and stormy days ahead. A committed prayer life enriched by the Holy Spirit's companionship will strengthen and sustain us daily.

Have you made a decision to trust Christ as your personal Savior? If your answer to this question is yes, then this chapter is written to be an encouragement and a reminder of just how personal and caring your Lord is! If your response is *no* or *not sure*, refer to the addendum at the close of this chapter, which explains the steps you can take for eternal security found only through Jesus Christ. It's a decision you won't regret!

Fruit of Purpose

The gift of salvation produces fruit—the fruit of purpose.

God's calling is full of incredible potential!

1. "On your mark…get set….go!!" This familiar charge signifies the start of a competition—specifically—a race. What two directives are given in Hebrews 12:1 that would enable the participant to accomplish the race set before them?

   ~   Let us _____.

   ~   Let us _____.

2. The weight referred to in Hebrews 12:1 is massive, actually bend-
    ing or bulging in its shape and position! How would such a hin-
    drance affect a teen's ability to stay on course?

    _____

    _____

    ~   What burdens are pressing upon you, preventing you from
        advancing forward in your spiritual walk with God?

        _____

3. One way to shed the unwanted baggage on our Christian journey
    is to maintain an attitude of cheerful endurance and hope. Paul
    states in Philippians 3:14, "I press toward the mark for the prize
    of the high calling of God in Christ Jesus." Bible Commentator
    Albert Barnes defines this calling for the Christian as one "from
    heaven and to heaven." In other words, our spiritual life-mission
    originates with the acceptance of a divine gift (the moment we
    are saved) and concludes with heavenly benefits (the moment we
    are united with Christ)!

    In the following verses, what words are used to describe this
    honorable goal?

    ~   1 Peter 1:4 _____

        _____

    ~   Colossians 1:5 _____

4. What can those who have completed this event expect to receive?
    (See 2 Timothy 4:7–8.)

    _____

    ~   Is anyone else eligible to receive the same reward?_____

~ For what additional reason?

_____

5. What can one who has endured temptation expect to receive in James 1:12?

_____

~ How is this individual described? _____

6. Psalm 119:1 states, "Blessed are the undefiled in the way, who walk in the law of the LORD." The Hebrew word used for way in this context means a course of life. We seem to keep coming back to the theme of being on a path—God's path! Can you see the purpose God has for those who "walk in the law of the Lord"? What attributes would be needed in order to perform this mode of action?

_____

7. Displaying on the outside what has taken place on the inside is what a God-centered testimony is all about! Have you heard the expression: "walks the talk"? It's one thing to be knowledgeable about spiritual matters; it's quite extraordinary to exhibit it on a daily basis! God clearly desires us to be useful during our time here on earth. Match the following verses with the description that best suits what God expects of us:

_____ 2 Corinthians 1:4   a. God wants us to do good works.

_____ Ephesians 2:10   b. We must be faithful.

_____ Galatians 6:1-2   c. We are equipped to comfort each other.

_____ 1 Corinthians 4:2   d. Be sensitive to other's burdens and trials.

~ Paul's encouraging words in 2 Timothy 1:9 tell us that God has saved us and called us to a holy life. This calling is a sacred invitation. He accepts us as we are and shows no preferential treatment. God's intentions for us are always pure! How does Romans 2:11 describe God's behavior towards us?

_____

_____

8. God's calling for us isn't based upon merit or good works. The second part of 2 Timothy 1:9 explains that it is not because of anything we have done, but according to His own purpose and grace. We may not always understand God's purpose for us, but we can be assured that it is always good and far-reaching! Who does the Lord shed His tender mercies and goodness upon in Psalm 145:9?

_____

9. Paul's concluding words in 2 Timothy 1:9 remind us that deliverance for our sins (Christ's substitution and power over death) was a deliberate, orderly plan set into motion before any of us ever came into being. God has arranged a miraculous way for us to be redeemed and found righteous in His eyes. However, it doesn't end there! As you write out Psalm 1:3 below, meditate on the results that come with having a secure foundation in Jesus Christ.

_____

_____

_____

_____

_____

Fruit of Prayer

The gift of salvation produces fruit—the fruit of prayer.

God's calling is very precious and very personal!

1. Perhaps the most unique privilege we acquire as a result of our newfound relationship in Christ is that of prayer. Our private thoughts, concerns, and fears can be freely shared, having the surety of our Father's confidence and care. What wording is used in these verses that demonstrates the emotional and expressive nature of prayer?

    ~ Psalm 28:2 _____

    ~ Psalm 61:1 _____

    ~ Psalm 62:8 _____

    ~ Psalm 119:171 _____

2. Think of prayer as our heavenly "hotline"—a 24/7 connection, with no busy-signals or annoying voicemail messages! God created us, cares for us, and takes a special interest in our lives. Refer to the following passages and record some of the reasons for our turning to God:

    ~ 2 Chronicles 7:14 _____

    ~ Psalm 4:1 _____

    ~ Jonah 2:7 _____

    ~ Matthew 26:41 _____

    _____

    ~ Romans 10:1 _____

3. It was Charles H. Spurgeon who once stated: "Prayer is the slender nerve that moves the arm of the Omnipotent." In James 5:16, prayer is described as effectual, which means it possesses power and energy. Our English word energy is derived from the Greek word *energeo*, which is used here. Imagine how victorious our Christian walk could be if we activated that force on a regular basis! Your prayers can make a difference!

~ In the chart below, note *who* is praying, *why* they are praying, and *how* prayer is used in their life.

	Who is praying?	Why is he/she praying and how is prayer used in his/her life?
Isaiah 38:1–5		
Daniel 4:34,37		
Jonah 2:1–3		

	Who is praying?	Why is he/she praying and how is prayer used in his/her life?
Luke 6:12–13		

4. One who is prayerful ACTS like it. ☺ The pattern for our quiet time with God, abbreviated with the acronym A.C.T.S., may include some or all of the following themes.

-   **Adoration:** praising God and exalting Who He is

-   **Confession:** admitting our guilt and asking God to completely absolve one of their sinful way(s)

-   **Thanksgiving:** thanking God for answered prayer, daily blessings and provision, etc.

-   **Supplication:** bringing before God our requests and burdens

    Can you identify which type of prayerful behavior is expressed?

    ~   Psalm 51:2 _____

    ~   Luke 1:46–47 _____

    ~   Numbers 21:7 _____

    ~   Psalm 95:1 _____

5. According to Isaiah 59:2 and Psalm 66:18, what prevents God from hearing our prayers?

    _____

~ Our prayers stand a better chance of being heard, if we keep our sin check-list short! When was the last time you were honest with the Lord, and acknowledged unconfessed sin in your life?

_____

~ I find that my day runs so much smoother when I begin it with a "clean slate." Try to regularly evaluate your motives and actions—remembering that God is patiently waiting to pardon your sin.

6. Who does 1 Timothy 2:5 identify as the mediator or "go-between" concerning man and God?

_____

~ Our prayers do not need to bypass through anyone other than Christ, and that's why we can claim Him as our **personal** Savior!

~ **Just for Fun**, go through the book of Psalms and write down as many of the metaphors (prefixed by "my") that are used to depict God (i.e., my Shepherd).

_____

_____

_____

7. Prayer is so beneficial! Being in His presence daily will not only challenge us to be holy (like Him), but an attitude of reverence will naturally accompany our spirit as well. What sweet fellowship is promised to those who are sincere and submissive in heart! Refer to Psalm 5:1–3 as you complete the following questions.

~ List the various ways the psalmist pleads for God's attention:

_____

_____

~ What time of day does the psalmist find suitable for prayer?

_____

~ How does the psalmist conclude verse 3?

_____

~ Why would it be important to pray in this manner?

_____

_____

~ Will you remember to pray with an expectant heart, one which has the confidence that God answers your prayers?

_____

8. This hymn piece, arranged by Pat Berg and Faye Lopez, beautifully summarizes our Savior's deep concern and sensitivity:

God Hears My Prayer
I bow on my knees before Him;
I come to my Lord in prayer.
Convinced of His love and mercy,
I bring my every care.
I pour out my heart before Him
Who knows my deepest fear.
In pity His arms surround me;
He wipes away each tear.

Chorus:
God hears my prayer when I come to Him in my darkest hour.
God hears my prayer when I bring to Him my need.
He'll lift me up, and He'll give me grace in trouble.
God hears my prayer; He will surely answer me
In humble submission falling,
Confessing my straying heart,
I run to my waiting Father;
Forgiveness He'll impart.
My heart thrills with adoration;

His glory fills my sight,
Amazed that my God would love me,
In me He would delight.

> Prayer is not a way of getting what we want, but the
> way to become what God wants us to be.

Fruit of Power

The gift of salvation produces fruit—the fruit of power.

God's calling is accompanied by the influence of His Holy Spirit.

1. Do you remember the television commercial that was repre-
    sented by an energetic drum-thumping rabbit? The marketing
    slogan—"It keeps going and going…"—became synonymous
    with the long-lasting usefulness of the item being pitched.
    Despite its reputation for endurance, the Energizer battery does
    eventually wear out! There is only one source of power that can
    "keep going and going"—that of the Holy Spirit, Who takes up
    residence in our hearts at the moment of our conversion.

    ~   Where does this power originate from? (See Psalm 62:11.)

    _____

    ~   According to Psalm 68:35, what else does God give His people?

    _____

2. Strength is closely identified with power and is often referenced
    in God's Word. Webster's Dictionary defines strength as "the
    power to resist an attack or a force." Paul's instructions for spiri-
    tual warfare are given in Ephesians 6:10–17. Refer to these verses
    and answer the following:

    ~   Who/what is the force we need to resist? _____

    ~   What is required of one going into a battle? _____

~ What wording used in verse 12 describes our unseen foe?

_____

_____

3. In the Old Testament verses below, identify when strength may also be necessary.

   ~ Isaiah 40:29 _____

   ~ Nahum 1:7 _____

4. Strength is power in action! Recall the illustration of the Energizer Bunny's incredible stamina? What kind of strength is mentioned in Isaiah 26:4?

   _____

   ~ How does Isaiah 40:28 highlight God's endurance?

   _____

   _____

5. When we are receptive to His truths and submit ourselves to His Will, God works in mighty ways we never fathomed! Philippians 4:13 is a great passage to commit to memory. As you write it out below, have confidence that His power is all you need.we

   _____

6. What powerful influence does the Holy Spirit have upon the disciples in Acts 4:31?

   _____

   _____

   ~ How bold or strong are you when it comes to sharing your faith with others?

   _____

~ When was the last time you put the power of the Holy Spirit into action and told someone about Jesus Christ?

_____

7. We can always lean on our Lord, Who will not fail us, forsake us, or forget us. He is the One who directs our steps. What promise does 2 Samuel 22:33 proclaim?

_____

~ How could focusing on the outcome of this statement help you to have more strength as a Christian witness?

_____

_____

_____

8. Read Paul's counsel to the members of the church in Corinth in 1 Corinthians 2:1–5. What ultimate message did Paul desire the people to comprehend?

_____

~ Paul mentions that he was experiencing weakness, fear and much trembling. Does this sound like a man who is strengthened by God?

_____

~ How was the power of the Holy Spirit demonstrated to Paul's audience?

_____

_____

_____

_____

_____

~ What would be the danger if the Corinthians' faith relied upon the wisdom of men, instead of the power of God?

_____

_____

_____

9. How do Paul's words in 1 Corinthians 2:1–5 confirm what Peter declares in 1 Peter 5:6?

_____

_____

_____

_____

Salvation = Purpose + Prayer + Power

Whether you have just begun your Christian walk as a new believer or have been traveling the path for some time, it's encouraging to know that God's plan for you is unique. It's a life-long progression of both opportunity and opposition, designed with a purpose, exclusively for you. How sure are you of this fact?

Philippians 1:6 promises, "Being confident of this very thing, that he which hath begun a good work in you will perform it until the day of Jesus Christ." Consider yourself a "work in progress"—the Master isn't done with you yet! Patiently and lovingly, as clay in the potter's hand, we are subjected to His control and care in our lives. He has fashioned you in His image, and is skillfully chipping away and smoothing out the rough spots.

Prayer, a vital tool in this relationship, strengthens us in our faith as we see God respond to our requests and needs. Salvation enables our Creator to equip us with supernatural power found in the person of the Holy Spirit. When difficulties arise, we have an advocate (supporter), the Lord Jesus Christ; we are not alone anymore!

Jesus' closing words in Matthew 28:20, "…And lo, I am with you always, even unto the end of the world," validate to His disciples that His presence is everlasting. We, as His children, can welcome this same divine assurance!

ADDENDUM
Have You Trusted Jesus Christ as Your Personal Savior?

In November of my senior year in high school, my grandmother suffered a stroke, which left her in a comatose state on life support. Up until that point, my faith in God had been rather superficial. However, a loved one was now suffering, and *that* reality brought me to my knees! I found myself desiring to be in God's presence, and chose to spend my lunch hour in the school's chapel room, praying for a miraculous healing.

My grandmother never recovered and passed away a few weeks later. I felt strangely at peace, comforted by the assurance that God knew what was best for her. Although the need was not as pressing as it had once been, I continued meeting with God every (school) day in that little chapel room. Graduation came in June, and I went on with my life . . . .

How I wish I had continued to heed God's calling in my life! For many years, I strayed from the faith, which is a polite way of saying that "I chose my way over God's way." My choices were certainly out of God's Will. I had ignored His goodness—even His very existence. How could He continue to love me despite my sinfulness and foolish pride?

How thankful I am that God did not give up on me! After years of ignoring His Word, God allowed the testimonies of several Bible-believing Christians to reach me with this certainty, "For by grace are ye saved through faith; and that not of yourselves: it is the gift of God; not of works, lest any man should boast." (Ephesians 2:8–9) I had a decision to make—whether or not to accept God's gift of salvation—and to accept it by faith and faith alone.

That late-night drive home in the car, was the beginning of a special and enduring relationship with my heavenly Father. I know that I am never alone, and that He will always be with me. My faith isn't based upon a feeling, but is rooted in the truths of His Word. I have the assurance of knowing that my eternal destiny is in heaven!

Despite God's attributes of Omnipotence (all-powerful), Omnipresence (all-present) and Omniscience (all-knowing), He gives us a free will to make this choice on our own. Yielding ourselves to His authority requires trust and a turning away from the old nature. There is a transformation that takes place, as stated in 2 Corinthians 5:17: "Therefore if any man be in Christ, he is a new creature: old things are passed away; behold, all things are become new." Inviting Christ into your life is personal—He wants to be Lord of your life! If you have not made a decision to trust Jesus Christ as your Lord and Savior, why not consider it today?

The steps to salvation are very basic, as easy as "ABC"…

A cknowledge that you are a sinner. God is righteous and perfect and holy. Sin cannot reside in His presence. There's a penalty for the sin debt we owe—the wages are death, eternal separation from God.

> **Romans 3:23** "For all have sinned, and come short of the glory of God;"

> **Romans 6:23** "For the wages of sin is death; but the gift of God is eternal life through Jesus Christ our Lord."

B elieve that Jesus Christ died for your sins, was buried, and rose again on the third day. His death was the perfect love sacrifice, claiming victory over death.

> **Romans 5:8** "But God commendeth his love toward us, in that, while we were yet sinners, Christ died for us."

> **1 Corinthians 15:3-4** "For I delivered unto you first of all that which I also received, how that Christ died for our sins according to the scriptures; And that he was buried, and that he rose again the third day according to the scriptures."

C onfess, asking forgiveness for your sin and trusting in Jesus' finished work on the cross. Pray sincerely, recognizing Jesus as the One who has saved you from your sins—past, present and future!

> **Romans 10:9–10** "That if thou shalt confess with thy mouth the Lord Jesus, and shalt believe in thine heart that God hath raised him from the dead, thou shalt be saved. For with the heart man believeth unto righteousness; and with the mouth confession is made unto salvation."

> **Romans 10:13** "For whosoever shall call upon the name of the Lord shall be saved."

Get alone with God and pray a prayer similar to this one*:

> Dear God, I know that I'm a sinner and deserve the punishment of hell. I believe that Jesus took my place on the cross and shed His blood for me. I ask you, Lord Jesus, to come into my heart and save me from my sins. From this time forward, I will try to live my life pleasing to you. Thank you for saving me. In your name I pray, Amen.

*If you have made this decision…Congratulations! Consider today your spiritual birthday! You are born-again! This is the most important decision you will ever make! Be sure to tell someone about the change that has taken place in your heart!

Fertilizing Your Spirit

Spiritual Growth

> Daily devotions......Attending a weekly woman's Bible study...Tithing......Lifestyle convictions.......Handing out tracts...... Teaching a Sunday school class......... Visitation....God certainly had a way of showing me the spiritual areas that needed attention and improvement!

How I wish I could declare that as a new believer I immediately began to pay heed to the various aspects of a Christ-centered life! It took some time for me to unravel the false doctrinal beliefs that had held me in spiritual bondage for so long. Yet, it was my desire to live for Christ that gradually repositioned my priorities and expectations.

As my baby steps began to gain momentum and stride, I became more conscious of the difference I could make upon others. For example, in 2002, when our youth minister asked me to consider teaching a girls' Sunday school class, I immediately thought, "*There is no way I could do that!*" Was I sincerely willing to trust God in this situation? I had a ton of excuses for why teaching the class would *not* work, but I couldn't get past the nagging feeling that God was taking me out of my comfort zone. (It wasn't the first time He had done that to me!) After much consideration and prayer, I said yes, choosing to recognize this as an opportunity, rather than an obstacle. Now *that* is spiritual growth!

Every garden is meant to be productive—why else would one put forth so much time and effort into its tending? Similarly, your spiritual garden needs daily maintenance in order to see evidence of fruit. As a disciple of Christ, is your spiritual tank being frequently replenished?

Can you echo the psalmist's sentiment in Psalm 63:1? "God, thou art my God; early will I seek thee: my soul thirsteth for thee, my flesh longeth for thee in a dry and thirsty land, where no water is." Our thirsty souls should eagerly and regularly be filled to capacity. As we abide in Him, we can expect to become more conformed to His image, fit for the Master's use. A spiritual diet equipped with the right ingredients will always result in dynamic growth!

Spiritual growth is stimulated by discipleship

1. The process of nurturing a seedling into a mature plant entails diligent care and attention, plus the expertise of a seasoned farmer. Spiritual growth requires the same special treatment. A more experienced (mature) Christian can be such an asset and a blessing to a new believer. Refer to these verses and identify who is the spiritual "care-taker" of a younger believer.

   ~ 1 Timothy 1:1–2 _____

   _____

   ~ Ruth 1:8, 14-16 _____

   _____

   ~ Titus 2:3-5 _____

2. Think of someone who has made an impact upon you concerning your spiritual walk with the Lord. What is it about this person that impresses you the most? Consider some of the following responses:

~ They are willing to take time and pray with me.

~ They are always encouraging me.

~ They are "real," not faking their Christianity.

~ They seem to have a lot of knowledge about the Bible.

~ Other: _____

~ How has this individual helped you to grow spiritually?

_____

3. In Deuteronomy 5:1, God uses Moses as His spokesperson to relay the Ten Commandments to the Israelites. What instructions are given to the people, concerning what they will hear?

_____

4. Discipleship could be defined as a period of time that a new Christian spends being instructed. Another name for a disciple is *pupil* or *student*, one who studies. What plea, spoken in Psalm 119:12, 26, and 64, shows an openness to learn?

_____

~ Referring to the same references, what should a disciple of Jesus desire to study?

_____

5. What characteristics mentioned in the following verses serve as a visible testimony of discipleship?

~ Matthew 5:16 _____

~ John 15:8 _____

~ John 8:31 _____

~ John 13:35 _____

6. The expression "bearing fruit" implies that growth has taken place. What instruction is commanded by Jesus in John 15:4–5?

_____

~ Describe the ways our connection with Christ is like the branches attached to the vine.

_____

_____

7. Write out John 15:16 here. _____

_____

_____

_____

~ The metaphor of the vine is used here and specifically describes our relationship as a secure and sheltered one. It is intended to be a productive position as well. How confident we can be, knowing that God's will for us is to be industrious, reaching others with the Good News!

8. This passage, taken from Psalm 1:1–3, depicts a beautiful illustration of the fruitfulness that results from a believer's close relationship with God.

"Blessed is the man that walketh not in the counsel of the ungodly, nor standeth in the way of sinners, nor sitteth in the seat of the scornful. But his delight is in the law of the LORD; and in his law doth he meditate day and night. And he shall be like a tree planted by the rivers of water, that bringeth forth his fruit in his season; his leaf also shall not wither; and whatsoever he doeth shall prosper."

~ Who are we advised to not associate with? _____

_____

~ What emphasis is placed upon the "Law of the Lord"?

_____

_____

~ What signs reveal that there is fruitfulness (evidence of God's blessings)?

_____

_____

9. As we develop a closer relationship (abiding) and show proof of it (bearing fruit), we bring glory and honor to our Heavenly Father. Take a moment to tell Him how thankful you are that He has chosen YOU and planted you in His loving care.

Spiritual growth is strengthened by diligence

1. What comes to mind when you hear the word "diligence"?

_____

~ Some synonyms for *diligent* are: industrious, attentive, conscientious.

~ Some antonyms for *diligent* are: careless, negligent, distracted.

~ If others were to describe your strengths, would "diligent" be on the top ten list of your best assets? Why or why not?

_____

_____

_____

_____

2. Diligence is a sign of a strong, consistent character. It is the effort one puts forth to accomplish a task (good or bad)—and to carry it out to fruition. Look up the following references and record your findings below:

	Who is showing diligence?	In what way?
Genesis 6:13–14, 22		
1 Samuel 23:14		
Matthew 2:1–2, 10–11		
Acts 2:42–47		

3. God's promise to give the land of Canaan to the seed of Abraham is finally a reality in Joshua 21:43–45. The Israelites now possess it and dwell safely therein. Yet, Joshua is quick to remind them of Moses' earlier instructions (spoken in Deuteronomy). In Joshua 22:5, his words emphatically declare that God's people "Take diligent heed . . ."

~ to _____.

~ to _____.

~ to _____.

~ to _____.

~ to _____.

4. What would be the danger in not being diligent with such counsel?

_____

_____

_____

_____

_____

5. Who does Proverbs 8:17 say "...shall find me"?

_____

_____

~ How would seeking Him early be an asset in spiritual growth?

_____

_____

6. In Psalm 63:1, David states that he will seek God early. What does David claim in the latter part of the verse?

   _____

   ~ What other outlook accompanied David's diligence?

   _____

7. David's description of a physical thirst and hunger characterizes our souls' intense longing for (spiritual) satisfaction. In the following verses, find the phrase that expresses a yearning for God's presence:

   ~ Psalm 42:1–2 _____

   ~ Psalm 119:131 _____

   ~ Psalm 130:6 _____

   _____

   ~ Luke 24:32 _____

8. When diligence is applied, growth naturally results. What better way to represent this growth than with the simile of foliage! Fill in the blanks, then answer the following questions:

   ~ **Psalm 92:12:** "The righteous shall flourish like the

   _____; he shall grow like a _____ in Lebanon."

   ~ **Psalm 52:8:** "But I am like a _____ in the house of God: I trust in the mercy of God for ever and ever."

   ~ What qualities describe a palm tree? _____

   _____

~ What qualities describe a cedar tree in Lebanon?

_____

_____

~ What qualities describe a green olive tree?

_____

_____

~ How useful would any of these trees be if diligence was not a factor in their development?

_____

_____

_____

_____

9. Spiritual growth is also portrayed by the productivity of a man who has been diligent and trusting. After reading Jeremiah 17:7–8, complete the chart, noting the comparisons.

Image/illustration used:	How does this help to produce a diligent work ethic?
A tree planted by water	
Spreading of roots	

Image/illustration used:	How does this help to produce a diligent work ethic?
Does not see (fear) the heat coming	
Presence of green leaves	
Is not anxious (in the year of the drought)	
Does not cease from yielding fruit	

As the masterful Gardener, God nurtures our thirsty souls with His loving grace and righteous wisdom. Soaking in His presence daily will stimulate spiritual growth. Make an early appointment to meet with Him each day—that will show diligence!

Spiritual growth is steered by dependence upon God

1. Spiritual growth is not something you notice right away—it sort of creeps up on you! You may not realize how much God has done in your life, until you are faced with a trial or tragedy that

challenges your faithfulness. There is newfound hope and confidence in a personal God Who will neither disappoint nor abandon you during a crisis! Read these passages and identify the circumstances or reasons given for God's intervention.

~ Deuteronomy 20:1–4 _____

_____

~ Psalm 6:2 _____

~ Psalm 55:22 _____

~ Psalm 56:3 _____

~ Nahum 1:7 _____

2. Once we have placed our trust in Jesus Christ as our Saviour, we have become joined to Him, facing a future bright with promise! Look up Colossians 2:6–7 and answer the following questions:

~ Your spiritual journey has begun! What does Paul command believers to do, once they have received Christ?

_____

~ What phrases are used to describe our "starting out" condition?

_____

~ Is this the condition of one who is firm or flabby? _____

~ Spiritual development has occurred due to instruction. It has also brought about consistency and confidence. What kind of attitude should naturally occur?

_____

_____

3. Just like a young child is helpless and immature, we, as spiritual babes in Christ, require support and direction. Look up the following verses and identify who is responsible for providing guidance:

   ~ Psalm 48:14 _____

   ~ John 10:11, 27 _____

   _____

   ~ John 16:13 _____

4. What does 1 John 5:7 say these three are? _____

   _____

   ~ Why do you think this is significant? _____

   _____

   _____

   _____

5. What is Jesus' instruction to His disciples in Matthew 16:24, Mark 8:34, and Luke 9:23?

   _____

   _____

   _____

   ~ In your own words, explain why obedience to this teaching would "steer" you into becoming more dependent upon God.

   _____

   _____

   _____

6. A dependence upon God will naturally develop once we surrender our desires and commit daily to observe His guidelines! Proverbs 3:5–6 is a popular and powerful promise which can strengthen and encourage us in times of unease or uncertainty. Write it out below.

_____

_____

_____

_____

7. The word *trust* is synonymous with dependence. Throughout God's Word, we can see how this attribute is woven into the lives of those who revere God. We are never alone; God is always with us. Often, it is during times of testing when God reassures us with the promise, "I will be with thee." Name those who hear this declaration from the Lord.

~ Genesis 26:3 _____

_____

~ Genesis 31:3 _____

_____

~ Exodus 3:12 _____

_____

~ Deuteronomy 31:23 _____

_____

~ Judges 6:16 _____

_____

8. Spiritual growth has taken place, when we display confidence (and not fear), when facing future uncertainties. God's presence is beautifully expressed through His written Word. Here are some examples.

    ~   Exodus 19:4 _____

        _____

    ~   Psalm 94:18 _____

    ~   Psalm 36:7 _____

    ~   Isaiah 42:6 _____

    ~   John 14:17 _____

    ~   Revelation 21:23 _____

        _____

9. Spiritual growth for a Christian is meant to be an active, lifelong progression.

    ~   What firm instruction is given in 2 Peter 3:8? _____

        _____

    ~   If you have been a Christian for any period of time, there should have been a gradual and steady maturing in your walk with God. Growing in grace and knowledge means developing Christ-likeness in your actions and attitudes. Have others seen that in your life?

        _____

10. What measures do you need to take in order to grow spiritually?

    _____

    _____

Spiritual Growth = Discipleship + Diligence + Dependence

There is a strong spiritual application between gardening and a vibrant testimony. Let me explain… when I first began to cultivate a vegetable garden, I was amateurish and inexperienced. I consulted a number of professionals (i.e. neighbors, garden/nursery workers) and once informed, was eager to begin. I purchased and I planted and I watered and I waited….

When the early signs of life began to sprout, I was so thrilled! Success at last! The fruits of my labor were abundant and delicious! The following season, I planted an even larger crop, expecting another successful harvest; however, this time, much of my produce was lacking in both quantity *and* quality. What had I done wrong? The result was minimal growth, because I had forgotten to fertilize!

Fertilize means *"to make able to produce much."* We have the potential to be productive for the Lord during our time on earth. At the moment of our conversion, we receive all the essential elements for a Christ-centered testimony, but, too often, we fail to nourish and maintain it properly. We neglect to fertilize our spirits.

Our responsibility is to employ the divine qualities listed in 2 Peter 1:3–7 and ensure that there is production. Increasing in the knowledge of our Lord Jesus Christ is the heartbeat of spiritual growth. The apostle Peter uses the word *abound* to describe this action: "For if these things be in you, and abound, they make you that ye shall neither be barren nor unfruitful in the knowledge of our Lord Jesus Christ." (2 Peter 1:8)

How would you describe your spiritual walk? Has your relationship with your Heavenly Father continued to thrive, or has it been in a state of idleness? Below are ten questions, which will help you assess your level of spiritual growth. Under each question, at least one Bible reference is given to support the action or attitude described. This list is intended for use as a guideline or resource tool. Be honest with yourself as you evaluate your personal relationship with God, then commit to "produce much" and strengthen those areas of weakness or apathy!

SPIRITUAL GROWTH CHECKLIST (KJV cited)

1. Am I rejoicing in the Lord daily? Do I reflect a joyful and thankful spirit?

   ~ Psalm 5:11 "But let all those that put their trust in thee rejoice: let them ever shout for joy, because thou defendest them: let them also that love thy name be joyful in thee."

   ~ Psalm 92:1 "It is a good thing to give thanks unto the LORD, and to sing praises unto thy name, O most High."

2. Am I living a life of obedience, pleasing the Lord in all that I do?

   ~ John 14:21 "He that hath my commandments, and keepeth them, he it is that loveth me: and he that loveth me shall be loved of my Father, and I will love him, and will manifest myself to him."

3. Are my motives pure and God-honoring? Am I seeking God's approval and not man's?

   ~ 1 Corinthians 10:31 "Whether therefore ye eat, or drink, or whatsoever ye do, do all to the glory of God."

   ~ 1 Corinthians 15:58 "Therefore, my beloved brethren, be ye stedfast, unmoveable, always abounding in the work of the Lord, forasmuch as ye know that your labour is not in vain in the Lord."

4. Is there any unconfessed sin blocking my communion with a Holy God?

   ~ Psalm 32:5 "I acknowledged my sin unto thee, and mine iniquity have I not hid. I said, I will confess my transgressions unto the LORD; and thou forgavest the iniquity of my sin."

   ~ Proverbs 28:3 "He that covereth his sins shall not prosper: but whoso confesseth and forsaketh them shall have mercy."

5. Is my attitude one of servant-hood?

   ~ Deuteronomy 10:12 "And now, Israel, what doth the LORD thy God require of thee, but to fear the LORD thy God, to walk in all his ways, and to love him, and to serve the LORD thy God with all thy heart and with all thy soul."

   ~ John 12:26 "If any man serve me, let him follow me; and where I am, there shall also my servant be: if any man serve me, him will my Father honour."

6. Do I recognize what God is doing in my life and share it with others?

   ~ 1 Samuel 12:24 "Only fear the LORD, and serve him in truth with all your heart: for consider how great things he hath done for you."

   ~ Psalm 77:12 "I will meditate also of all thy work, and talk of thy doings."

7. Am I spending time, on a daily basis, reading and meditating upon His Word?

   ~ Joshua 1:8 "This book of the law shall not depart out of thy mouth; but thou shalt meditate therein day and night, that thou mayest observe to do according to all that is written therein: for then thou shalt make thy way prosperous, and then thou shalt have good success."

   ~ Psalm 119:16 "I will delight myself in thy statutes: I will not forget thy word."

8. Do I pray according to His Will?

   ~ 1 John 5:14 "And this is the confidence that we have in him, that, if we ask any thing according to his will, he heareth us."

   ~ Psalm 143:1 "Hear my prayer, O LORD, give ear to my supplications: in thy faithfulness answer me, and in thy righteousness."

9. Do I allow myself to be used of God? Is my response a humble one?

   ~ Philippians 2:13 "For it is God which worketh in you both to will and to do of his good pleasure."

   ~ James 4:10 "Humble yourselves in the sight of the Lord, and he shall lift you up."

10. Do I spend time praising/worshipping Him?

    ~ Psalm 7:17 "I will praise the LORD according to his righteousness: and will sing praise to the name of the LORD most high."

    ~ Psalm 111:1 "Praise ye the LORD. I will praise the LORD with my whole heart, in the assembly of the upright, and in the congregation."

Harvest Time!

Witnessing

> In the months leading up to my conversion, I worked for a Christian supervisor named Dana. I had never met anyone like Dana before. He would keep a Bible on his desk, talk openly about the Lord, and praise Him unashamedly. His Christianity was genuine and, wow, was it ever contagious!

There was no mistaking that Dana loved God and wanted to share that news with everyone! I thought Dana's conduct was a bit peculiar, yet he always seemed to display a cheerful and kind character despite the pressures or problems he encountered. Dana's unconventional behavior possessed a distinctive....essence.

What do you think of when the word *essence* is mentioned? I think of smells—perhaps the fragrance of blossoming lilacs....a juicy steak on the grill....the clean, crisp smell of laundered sheets.... Each of these conjure up an immediate and recognizable odor that would distinguish it from any another object. Just like each of these items has a characteristic scent, we as Christians have a fragrance (our essence) that identifies us. And whether we are conscious of it or not, we are spreading an aroma wherever we go!

Similarly, witnessing (telling others about Christ) symbolizes a scent-saturated presence that will stir up a reaction! Notice the two extreme responses to the Christian's "odor" in 2 Corinthians 2:15–16:

"For we are unto God a sweet savour of Christ, in them that are saved, and in them that perish. To the one we are the savour of death unto death; and to the other the savour of life unto life." When we talk about the Lord with others, it is Good News to some (the savor of life); but repulsive to others (the savor of death).

Nonetheless, spreading the news about Jesus' death, burial, and resurrection is a command. God will ultimately bless those who have obediently followed His will to "Go ye into all the world, and preach the gospel to every creature" (Mark 16:15). Our mission is meant to be a joyous one, relying upon His precious promises of hope and security. Are you willing to serve your God and be a testimony to a lost and dying world? The rewards of following Christ are immeasurable, as are the blessings we can expect in heaven for being found trustworthy and true.

Reap Rewards of Obedience

1. The command to spread the "good news" in Matthew 28:19 is known as the Great Commission. God's instruction for soul-winning involves having a global perspective. One way to fulfill this commitment is through evangelistic ministries. What obstacles do you believe a missionary faces when taking the gospel message into a foreign country?

   _____

   _____

   ~ What obstacles would a teen encounter when attempting to share Christ with non-believers?

   _____

   _____

   _____

~ How often do you pray for those who are serving in the mission field?

_____

2. Before we can witness to others, we have to first understand how God views us. How are we described in Romans 8:16–17?

_____

~ 1 Corinthians 3:9 _____

_____

~ 2 Corinthians 6:4 _____

~ Are we alone in this venture? _____

~ How would knowing that you are not alone in this special assignment give you confidence to obey Him?

_____

3. Sharing Christ is often depicted in terms of farming/vegetation. For example, sowing and planting seeds is illustrative of telling someone the news of Jesus' death, burial, and resurrection. According to 1 Corinthians 3:8, what two actions exerted are described as one?

_____

~ Describe one who plants. _____

_____

~ Describe one who waters. _____

_____

~ Who gives the increase? (See 1 Corinthians 3:7.) _____

4. After a seed has been planted and watered, we can expect it to naturally germinate or sprout. So it is with the gospel. What does God expect us to do in John 15:16 ?

———————————————————

   ~ What is promised to those who have sown righteousness in Proverbs 11:18?

———————————————————

5. When we respond appropriately to what the Lord commands, we can expect something extraordinary to take place! One such example is illustrated in Acts 8:26–35, which depicts the conversion of the Ethiopian eunuch. Read the passage, then answer the following question:

   ~ An unusual command is spoken by the angel of the Lord, directing Philip to go south to Gaza. The area is described as desert, which makes the request seem rather futile. What is Philip's response in verse 37?

———————————————————

———————————————————

6. Once Philip arrives at the destination, he encounters a man from Ethiopia, returning from Jerusalem where he had gone to worship. How is this man described?

———————————————————

   ~ What was the eunuch doing in his chariot?

———————————————————

   ~ What does the (Holy) Spirit tell Philip to do next?

———————————————————

7. What is Philip's immediate response in verse 30?

_____

~ Philip's response is one of urgency and total compliance. Summarize the events that take place next.

_____

_____

8. Philip's obedience to the prompting of the Holy Spirit demonstrates the power of God and how effective it is (fruitfulness) when we serve Him wholeheartedly.

~ How productive have you been as a righteous servant of Christ?

_____

~ Are you seizing opportunities to tell others about what God has done in your life?

_____

9. When we strive to follow the Lord in an obedient manner, we will reap untold rewards. Proverbs 12:12 claims that the root of the righteous will yield fruit; no more troublesome weeds to threaten and destroy our outgrowth!

~ There *will* be fruit resulting from your faithful efforts to plant seeds and nurture souls for the kingdom of God! As you write out Proverbs 11:30 below, meditate on its simplistic, insightful message.

_____

_____

_____

Reap Rewards of His Promises

1. The easiest way to identify a promise in the Scriptures is to recognize that a promise from God is a fact. We can confidently proclaim His truths, realizing that He personally endorses every one of them! The future is bright, knowing that we have security and victory with God on our side. Should we fear how others will respond to the truths we desire to share? Why/Why not?

    _____

    _____

    _____

    _____

    ~   Describe a time when you were anxious about sharing your faith with someone.

        _____

        _____

    ~   Were there any promises from God's Word that helped you deal with this fearfulness or lack of confidence?

        _____

        _____

2. Witnessing (taking the gospel message to the unsaved) is not always a comfortable task, but it is an additional and fundamental display of spiritual growth. I've heard it said that faith is like a muscle; it needs to be exercised and stretched in order to be strengthened. When sharing our faith is not practiced on a routine basis, our spiritual "muscles" become flabby. Exercising the muscle of faith requires trusting in God's promises.

What is being promised in these verses?

~ Isaiah 26:3 _____

~ Psalm 86:7 _____

~ Psalm 31:24 _____

~ Matthew 11:29 _____

~ Romans 10:9 _____

~ 1 John 1:9 _____

3. God's promises will also give us confidence! Philippians 4:13 proclaims, "I can do all things through Christ which strengtheneth me." What spiritual areas listed below need strengthening in your life?

~ _____ Prayer

~ _____ Bible-reading/devotions

~ _____ Witnessing/Soul-winning

~ _____ Faithfulness (to church services or Sunday school)

~ _____ Serving

~ _____ Having a better testimony around others

~ _____ Tithing /Giving

4. Our personal relationship with our heavenly Father will deepen as we see Him act on our behalf. He is our advocate, generous in wisdom, and always attentive to our needs. What promise concerning His responsiveness is declared in 1 John 5:14?

_____

5. How would being familiar with God's abundant promises help you to become a more effective witness for Christ?

_____

_____

_____

6. God's promise to strengthen us can provide all the stamina we need in order to serve Him. Galatians 6:9 advises us to "not be weary in well doing." What is promised to those who have persisted?

_____

~ God has appointed the proper time, "*in due season*," in which to give a reward, the result, or—as in gardening terms—the harvest. The principle of sowing and reaping means we can expect a return with our investment. We must continue to trust in God's perfect timing!

7. A profound statement about God's sovereignty is given in Ecclesiastes 3:14. What does this verse claim about God's character?

_____

~ How would this reality give you the courage you need to witness?

_____

8. Believing in the promises of God's Word means we have something to look forward to. What promise can we anticipate in 1 John 2:25?

_____

9. What promise, stated twice in Hosea 2:19, accompanies the reward promised in 1 John 2:25?

_____

10. God views us as his betrothed. *Betrothed* is an obsolete vocabulary term, rarely used in twenty-first century dialogue. A more contemporary expression would be "engaged" or "bride-to-be," symbolic of future promise and unity. What beautiful imagery to describe our value to God and position in Christ!

> The union that awaits us, where we are *betrothed* to Him forever!
> It is a marriage vow that will never be broken;
> A celebration that will never cease;
> Christ is coming again for us—to return for His bride;
> And to fulfill His best promise of all!

~ Are you excited about this future promise? Are you telling others about it?

Reap Rewards of Joyfulness

1. For your testimony to be "sweet," it has to radiate joyfulness. What other characteristics could be included to describe someone who is joyful?

_____

_____

~ Notice that joy is included with a cluster of character traits—the "fruit" of the Spirit found in Galatians 5:22–23. List them here:

_____

_____

2. Refer to these passages and identify what can bring us joy.

   ~ Psalm 118:24 _____

   ~ Psalm 119:162 _____

   ~ Psalm 139:14 _____

   _____

3. What do Psalm 13:5 and Psalm 35:9 mention as a source of praise?

   _____

   ~ What causes the psalmist to rejoice greatly in Psalm 71:23?

   _____

   ~ What does it mean to be redeemed? _____

   ~ Look the definition up and write it here. _____

   _____

4. Man's corrupt nature is often characterized as something which has gone astray or been misplaced, in need of deliverance. What words could be used to describe this wayward condition?

   _____

   _____

   _____

5. In Luke 15:4–9, Jesus shares two parables with a mixed crowd of Pharisees and scribes (the religious people of the day) and publicans and sinners (social outcasts). What items of significance are "lost"?

_____

~ What does the "lost-ness" represent in these parables?

_____

_____

~ What measures were taken to find what was lost?

_____

_____

_____

~ What was their response once the lost item was found?

_____

_____

6. Notice that both individuals in the parable of the lost sheep and the lost coin make a point of saying, "Rejoice with me!" Oh! The exuberance that follows after one has found Christ—or rather, been found by Christ. This type of joy demands fellowship, a mutual expression of support and security! When was the last time you rejoiced over a new believer's decision to accept Jesus Christ as their personal Savior?

_____

~ Who else rejoices *with us* when a sinner is saved? (See verses 7 and 10.)

_____

7. We who have experienced the forgiveness of God through His glorious plan of redemption, should naturally desire it for our loved ones. Great delight will come to those who have been faithful to pray and tell others about Christ. Psalm 126:5 promises, "They that sow in tears shall reap in joy."

~ Explain what it means to "sow in tears."

_____

_____

~ Do you faithfully pray for those you know who need Jesus Christ as their Savior? Name some of them here.

_____

_____

~ List ways in which you can testify to others about the saving grace God freely gives.

_____

_____

_____

_____

8. Joyfulness should be the trademark of a Christian teen's testimony. As you fill in the blanks, notice the source that kindles a joyous spirit.

~ Nehemiah 10:8 "... for the _____ of the LORD is your strength."

~ Psalm 5:11 "But let all those that put their trust in thee

_____: let them ever shout for _____, because thou defendest them: let them also that love thy

name be _____ in thee."

~ Psalm 16:11 "Thou wilt shew me the path of life: in thy pres-

ence is _____; at thy right hand there are plea-

sures for evermore."

~ Isaiah 61:10 "I will greatly _____ in the LORD, my

soul shall be _____ in my God; for he hath clothed
me with the garments of salvation, he hath covered me with
the robe of righteousness, as a bridegroom decketh himself
with ornaments, and as a bride adorneth herself with her
jewels."

~ Philippians 2:16 "Holding forth the word of life; that I may

_____ in the day of Christ, that I have not run in
vain, neither laboured in vain."

9. Did you realize that God takes great delight in us as well? God
looks upon each one of us as unique and valuable. Look up these
verses and record the pleasures God sees in us.

~ Genesis 1:31

_____

~ Psalm 104:31

_____

~ Proverbs 11:20 _____

_____

~ Isaiah 62:5 _____

_____

~ Jude 1:24 _____

_____

Someday soon we will be reunited with the One who loves us unconditionally, the One who has prepared an eternal, glorious home for us, the One who has brought our soul out of bondage and redeemed us. This wonderful reunion with our Redeemer and Maker is described in Isaiah 51:11. Read it with anticipation and joy! We will reap the bountiful blessings that await us in eternity! Everlasting joy is promised to those who have trusted in the Savior. Who will you share Christ with today?

Witnessing = Obedience + Promises + Joyfulness

"Well-done, good and faithful servant": what powerful words of approval are spoken in Matthew 25:23, signifying sanctified behavior and a righteous heart! *Well-done* means we have been willing, and that our accomplishment has brought much delight to our heavenly Father. Is there anything else in our lives that should muster such high regard?

The greatest joy we can experience is to communicate to others the saving grace that awaits them. The blessings are abundant and the rewards plentiful for those who have been found faithful and true. The invitation to "enter thou into the joy of thy lord" (Mark 25:23b) is an exclusive and exceptional appeal. It should excite us to be reaching out to the lost, being busy about the Lord's work. The exact realization of this goal will ultimately be found in His eternal presence!

The reward for being a faithful witness is found in the principle of sowing and reaping. Whether we channel our efforts into being a sower (one who plants/shares the gospel) or a reaper (one who leads a soul to Christ), our duty is to actively respond to the task God directs us to do. Learn to rely upon God's wisdom—He truly knows what is best for each one of us. Allow your testimony as a Christian to shine and show the world that you are a child of God! "But sanctify the Lord God in your hearts: and be ready always to give an answer to every man that asketh you a reason of the hope that is in you with meekness and fear"(1 Peter 3:15).

AFTERWORD

As I completed this Bible study, the Lord reminded me of a more recent flashback. It didn't take place during my teenage years, nor did it occur in the early years of my adult life. It was, however, the result of much prayer, many shed tears, and the readiness to share the gospel with one lost soul:

December 19, 2006 is a day I wish I could have turned back the clock. My father was involved in a serious car accident that day, one which left him paralyzed from the neck down.

Unfortunately, I couldn't rush right over. Due to my husband's job relocation eight months earlier, our family now lived over 400 miles away. I was unable to visit him as much as I would have liked to. All I could do was pray.

So I did.

Looking back, I see how God's Hand was directing the whole scenario. My dad needed the Lord, and it wasn't until he was bed-bound, unable to walk and function normally that God got his attention.

I was able to drive down for a four-day visit in early March. I realized that this might be the last time I would ever see my dad alive. His condition had begun to deteriorate.

I had been praying for my father's salvation for nearly twenty years, ever since I came to know the Lord. There had been opportunities, but this time was different. The burden was greater; the urgency more pressing.

The Lord would work it out (you probably know that this flashback has a good ending ☺).

When I arrived at the nursing home with my two young daughters, my mother was quick to scoot out and take them on a shopping spree. Little did she know that the time alone with Dad would be invaluable!

Over the next few days (and repeated Grandmom/granddaughter shopping ventures), I had the chance to discuss many topics with Dad. What do you think heaven is like? Are you angry with God? What were you taught as a little boy? These were some of the most cherished discussions I experienced and will never forget.

On Sunday morning, I attended the worship service at my former church, Open Bible Baptist Church in New Jersey. I remember going to the altar that morning with my dear friend Lori and weeping for my Dad's conversion. Today HAD to be the "day of his salvation."

God gave me great peace that day, as well as great boldness. I was on a mission. I felt strong and confident, knowing that the words I spoke were that of the Holy Spirit.

It was a very basic conversation between a father and daughter. Yet, I was speaking to one of a child-like faith—my own father!

"Dad, I have to leave tomorrow. I'm not sure when I will see you again."

"Dad, we are all going to die someday."

"Did you know that you can make a decision now, in this life that will determine where you will go after you die?"

"I know that when I die, I am going to heaven! So is Ted, and our children!"

"Do you want to know how you can be sure of the same fact, Dad?"

A pause.

Then, a firm nod of his head, conveying the invite to continue with the presentation of the Good News! Oh! What precious Good News it is!

Eyes wide and blue, looking directly into mine: "Yes. Yes, I would, Karen!"

Halleluiah! Praise the Lord! Thank you, Jesus!

It just all sort of gushed out of me: John 3:16, Romans 3:23, Romans 6:23, Romans 5:8, and Romans 10:13. The wonderful words of life! The redemption promised through the shed blood of God's Only Son. It never loses its power…

As I recall the moment even now, the tears I shed are those of great joy and relief! I know that Dad accepted Christ as His personal Savior that day, and I give all the glory to God!

A few weeks later, my dad passed away. What reassurance I had, knowing that he was home in heaven!

Later, my sister made a comment that she thought a loving God

should not have allowed Dad to suffer; that it would have been more merciful of God to take Dad immediately on the day of the accident.

I told her about Dad's decision and the assurance I had about his salvation.

She replied, "I know. When I asked him how his visit went with you, he told me that you and he prayed together."

Dad knew that there was something extraordinary about the prayer he prayed that day with me; that the confession of sin and the acceptance of a Savior into the heart was a promise that would last for all eternity!

"Behold, I stand at the door, and knock: if any man hear my voice, and open the door, I will come in to him, and will sup with him, and he with me" (Revelation 3:20).

Group Leader's Guidelines

Objectives for this study:

1. This material is intended to be used as a weekly curriculum for Sunday School or small group Bible study for Junior and Senior high school girls (7th–12th grades).

2. A Bible is required to reference the quoted Scripture and to be used as a reference source/tool for the questions posed. The authorized King James Version of the Bible has been used exclusively.

3. Each chapter begins with a brief flashback incident. The example is based upon a true-to-life account that the author experienced in her teen/young adult years. It is meant to be a good starting point for discussion of the chapter's theme. Encourage participation and feedback, referring to the theme often.

4. Prior to beginning Chapter 1, the teacher needs to introduce the the questionaire. This quiz can help identify the problem areas that are addressed later in the study. An answer key is included.

5. Most of all—pray for your girls! God has given you a wonderful opportunity to be the spokeswoman for a Bible study which may drastically change their lives! Don't take it lightly! Many teen girls want help dealing with the various "issues" in their lives, but won't seek it on their own. With God's help, they can develop firm convictions and grow closer to Him . . . isn't that what we all want?

Before you get started:

1. **Guidelines/suggestions:** The symbolism of vegetation is used as an easy means of comparison throughout this study. Your teen girl audience should quickly recognize the application of the "What Kind of Fruit are You?" quiz. Prior to distributing the quiz to the girls, consider the following:

   - This quiz is in no way intended to be a definitive diagnosis for any ongoing issues a teen girl may be struggling with. It is meant to aid in the identification of what "weed areas" have taken up root.

   - Stress the confidentiality of the quiz-taking process. Many of the statements are personal. In order for the girls to be honest with themselves, it is important that they are not influenced by feedback or remarks that could sway their choices.

   - There are no right or wrong answers. Each statement requires a subjective answer relying upon the sole opinion and knowledge of the quiz-taker.

   - Encourage the girls to thoroughly understand the intent of the statement before circling their response. If they need you to define a word, use a dictionary.

   - Explain that because of our sin nature, we *all* are guilty of the various topics being addressed in the quiz categories. It would be wonderful to score a low point value, but it is not very realistic!

2. **Additional facts:** The connection between assigning a fruit/veggie to a particular weakness in one's testimony took on a creative life of its own! I think it decreases the amount of intimidation that a teen girl may have about the topic of a good/bad testimony; and I believe identifying the problem ahead of time will be more of an asset when working on the material. Here are some additional facts that can be mentioned when discussing the quiz results:

- **Apple:** Chosen to represent **Purity**. Often, an apple will appear healthy and tasty on the outside, but its inner core may contain rottenness or a worm! One bad apple in the fruit basket affects the rest—it's never the other way around. Although the fruit Adam and Eve partook of is not specified in the Genesis account, an apple is commonly presented as the culprit.

- **Beans**: Chosen to represent **Hypocrisy.** This popular trait has been noted amongst the various strains of this vegetable. My initial gardening venture was marked by the mysterious presence of an unrecognizable sapling. It turned out that the "beans" that I had thought were string/pole beans turned out to be lima beans instead!

- **Carrots**: Chosen to represent **Wrong Influences.** Ever notice a crooked carrot? An obstacle (rock, chunk of wood, etc.) got in the way, causing its taproot to take a detour! Wrong influences in a teen's life are similar, causing one to "bend away" from the path of righteous behavior.

- **Coconut:** Chosen to represent **Authority Issues.** What a tough shell to crack! Teens struggling with authority issues may be just as difficult to deal with. The coconut is the largest seed known, and has the ability to float, enabling it to drift and plant itself on islands all over the tropical seas! It also takes a full year for a coconut to mature.

- **Grapes:** Chosen to represent **Peer Pressure.** Grapes aren't grown singularly—they are always bunched in clusters. It is the most frequently mentioned plant in the Bible. A grape vine cannot produce grapes unless it is pruned. There are over 600 varieties of grapes.

- **Lemon:** Chosen to represent **Having the Right Responses**. We've all heard the expression: "When life hands you a lemon, make lemonade." We *can* control our responses to exhibit either a sweet (good) or sour (bad) temperament.

- **Onion:** Chosen to represent **(Dis)Contentment.** Everyone is familiar with what happens when slicing and dicing an onion—tears! Discontentment is a highly emotional reaction, wallowing in pity and disappointments, and generating pessimism.

- **Peach:** Chosen to represent **Tongue Misuse.** The juicy drippings of this product mimic the ripeness of and desire for gossip. Peaches shouldn't be squeezed because they bruise easily—our words can do similar damage.

- **Watermelon:** Chosen to represent **Selfishness.** The large, curvy vine of the watermelon can grow to be over eight feet long. The largest watermelon ever grown is mentioned in the 1998 edition of the Guinness World Book of Records; it weighed 262 pounds!

3. **Additional Resources:** Group leaders and/or participants can visit **www.preceptpublishing.com** to download the answer key for the *Is Your Fruit Sweet or Sour?* Bible Study.

References

Knight, George W. *The Illustrated Guide to Bible Customs and Curiosities*, Barbour Publications, 2007.

Phil Lindner, Power BibleCD version 4.0a, Online Publishing, Inc., copyright 1999-2003.

Strong, James, LL.D., S.T.D. *The New Strong's Exhaustive Concordance of the Bible*, Thomas Nelson Publishers, 1990.

Pentz, Croft M. *The Complete Book of Zingers*, Tyndale House Publishers, Inc., Carol Stream, IL, 1990.

Hutson, Curtis. *Punch Lines*, Sword of the Lord Publishers, Murfreesboro, TN, 1989.

Karen Finn is not a best-selling author, but she wouldn't mind if that became a part of her portfolio someday! After years of freelance writing for both secular and Christian publications, Karen bravely ventured into the world of self-publishing, and Precept Publishing was born!

Karen has been involved in youth and women's ministries for more than 20 years. As she became more familiar with teaching teen girls, Karen developed a desire to see more fundamental material provided for young women. *Is Your Fruit Sweet or Sour?* is the result of that burden—it is her first published book.

Born and raised in Philadelphia, Karen resides in rural northwestern Pennsylvania with her husband, Ted, and their five young adults (ages 14 through 23).

CPSIA information can be obtained at www.ICGtesting.com
Printed in the USA
LVOW01s1108010814

397093LV00010B/116/P